RELATIONAL GOD

Jill Boyton

ACKNOWLEDGEMENTS

I would like to acknowledge the encouragement and belief I have received from my dear friends Heather and Lynda, who have read, prayed and enthused over every line of this book. Also, Jamie who gave up his time to critique and correct the copy, but most of all my love and thanks to my dearest husband who supported and helped me every step of the way.

THE HOLY BIBLE, NEW INTERNATIONAL VERSION®, NIV® Copyright © 1973, 1978, 1984, 2011 by Biblica, Inc.™ Used by permission. All rights reserved worldwide.

DEDICATION

To Roger, all my children and grandchildren, I dedicate this book to you. In reading it I hope you will understand what I have always believed to be true, I have no worldly treasure to leave as a legacy, but know that the knowledge of Jesus Christ is greater than any wealth, or accolade we can hand down to our family. And so with love and thanks I leave this book for you to read, thanking God for the joy you have given to me.

PREFACE

It has been my impression throughout the years that many of my fellow Christians have struggled with their beliefs due to their lack of understanding of the relationship available to us with the individual members of the Trinity, their own personality and purpose in our lives. Without this understanding we're hindered from entering fully into the fullness of being the children of the living God.

Even when committing our lives to the Lord Jesus and accepting His saving grace from our sins, we often don't understand that we have available to us interaction with all the Godhead now being part of their family, just as with our own earthly family. The depth of our faith will be amazingly extended when we understand the personal reason for God's desire for us to be obedient and live in faith of His care. Instead of 'we should' or 'must' being the motivation we act on, knowing the heart of our maker, desire becomes the thrust of our fellowship with Him.

I hope giving a brief overview of the components of this relationship will help. Of course it would take far too long to spell out all that is to be known, and indeed that would eradicate the very thing I hope to promote as the reading of scripture should be personal to each of us, and probably bring a deeper insight each time it is read.

To come to the realisation that we have a God who not only wants to know and interact with us, He wants us to know Him. I realise that not everyone has a loving and healthy relationship with their parents and family. Nevertheless, it is now our right and God's desire for us to feel we belong to Him and know the overarching love, care and desire He has for us. With this knowledge, we can fly. We can reach into the purposes that God has planned for us.

I do hope you'll gain excitement as you navigate your way through this book, deeper into the Love of God.

CONTENTS

Introduction..7

Part 1
Relationship with the Father...................13
Relationship with Jesus............................39
Relationship with the Holy Spirit...........73

Part 2
Truth of the Matter..................................91
Is it Fair?..111
A Question of Belief...............................135

Part 3
Home Straight..156
Last but not Least...................................170
The Conclusion......................................188

About the Author...................................196

INTRODUCTION

There's no room for God in my life.
I don't see any evidence of the existence of God.
If God exists, He's cruel and uncaring.
Belief in gods causes division and wars.
I believe in enlightenment through multiple faiths.
Religion has been used to manipulate and control.
When I die I go six foot under.
Man doesn't need a god to be good.
I believe in the big bang.
The Bible – a book that can't be proven.

You can probably add your own comments to the list above.

Gods have always been the centre of man's thinking. Maybe not the god we wish to follow now, but a higher power with which man has desired to connect with through all manner of religious practices and beliefs. These paths have undoubtedly had tremendous power whether through witch doctors or the hierarchy of church foundations. Not strange then that we're cautious or dismissive, even scathing if a so called truth is presented to us. I have believed for some time that the reason so many turn away from God is because of two main issues.

The first is that we don't fully understand the relational side of God's nature and how that affects us. Second, the whole idea of righteousness and the implications that has for us. This relational and righteous God is who I believe Jesus sought to unveil to all those who desire and dare to seek. Having to write with this in mind, I had better clear a few things up at the outset so hopefully the heart of the book can be seen through a different set of lenses.

For years, church for many has depicted God through the medium of stained glass windows, candles and bells, etc. Although there is a certain value in this, in the cold light of day it doesn't bring us closer to understanding the relevance of believing in God and what difference that makes to our lives.

Watching a series on TV exploring society in Tudor times, it was interesting but mind boggling to contemplate not only the way people lived but what was acceptable to them. The vast majority couldn't read, were massively superstitious and their practices were, to us, barbaric. Yet they believed in God. How on earth then could we make out what society after Adam and Eve could have been like?

That is, of course, if you choose to believe there was an Adam and Eve! However, the Bible does tell us a lot about the person of God.

We know God's DNA is righteousness and therefore anything that is less that righteous cannot coexist with Him. We believe God's nature is love and He created us to be like Himself. Therefore, those aspects of human nature that display love, originate from Him. We know He has emotions and is not detached from feeling. He desires relationship with us and is patient and forgiving. He certainly loves a celebration, but most of all He is a parent who is prepared to sacrifice that which is worth most to keep His children as part of His family.

In general, God gets a bad press and everything that's evil is laid at His door. It is quite ironic really when it is us that feel cross when everything God tells us to do is regarding as right. Such as loving your neighbour, turning the other cheek, and telling the truth. Why is that? Well if you were an adversary wouldn't you want to discredit your opponent? Every religion recognises there are two powers battling it out in life, one that stands for good and the other evil. Part of our misunderstanding is caused when we read scripture. We tend to use a harsh voice when God speaks. In every day life we can do this, making a request sound like an order for instance. But God says, "Don't do that, because you will get hurt." God does not need to bark out orders. He is peaceable, but His Word stands.

Let us not be unaware, this righteousness is a mighty force. Its power can create or destroy. God cannot be underestimated and He is 'The Truth'. What is more, to keep all that power intact, righteousness cannot be compromised. To say that I have a relationship with this great Almighty God is like saying I can have a relationship with the Treasurer of the Bank of England, when I struggle to manage my housekeeping. It is by His grace that I can interact with Him.

Do you watch the Antiques Roadshow? I love seeing the faces of those who bring in something which appears quite ordinary, then they are told it is some ancient antiquity which is worth a mint. Wouldn't we love to find some old thing like that in the loft! The show's experts are very shrewd and sometimes what appears to be a masterpiece turns out to be a worthless copy. Righteousness is a bit like that. If unspoilt it is priceless and powerful. What if it weren't authentic, like some of those paintings, and someone else had a hand in it? There would be no value in the painting. Could the expert excuse the counterfeit or would it render all the works of the artist dubious? God cannot be compromised or turn a blind eye to wrongdoing. His righteousness and holiness cannot be blurred by anything that might put His authenticity in jeopardy. However, God's righteousness works for our good, if only we obey Him. Although, we find this almost impossible to do. Amazingly though, He does provide a way out, bearing the cost to Himself.

I can remember when 'cause and effect' began to be accepted – now it is called 'Karma'. It is not a new concept. In fact, it's one God warned about from the start. You do good things and good will result, you do bad things and bad things will result. The confusion is that you don't always 'see' what is happening, but appreciate the effects later on. Many laws are passed to try and solve problems which have been caused because we have turned away from what God tells us is the right thing to do.
No one says it's easy. God knows that. In fact, it's a battle. He will be the commander of the army if only we will let Him. These two concepts which

make up God's character appear complex and contradictory but are necessary to understand what type of person God is. Would we want Him to be different? Where would we stand if He suddenly showed He was flawed? No, God can keep His integrity and give us our free will.

When bringing up my children, I often bought their bits and pieces from a catalogue. We didn't have much money so this was a helpful way to accommodate our budget. One time we had decided to buy a tent and the catalogue had a reasonably priced ridge tent advertised. When it arrived there was a mistake in the packing and although the invoice was for a ridge tent the actual tent was a better and a more expensive model. Here was the temptation. I could quite easily keep the tent and think I had a lucky break, or send it back and have the model I was actually entitled to. Everyone said "keep it!", but my father said, "You do what you think is right, but I know what I would do". I sent it back. Not only was my integrity intact, but my love and pride in my father's honesty increased massively. So I lost the tent, but gained a prize. This is an example of the foundation of the following. I hope it will help you navigate your way through to the end.

PART ONE

RELATIONSHIP WITH THE FATHER

Starting at the beginning.

If we were to look subjectively at what makes life tick from the bottom up, we would probably agree that relationship is the defining part of who we are and what is important to us. Relationship takes in the lights and shades of life, and when we try to work out what relationships have shaped us most, we might come up with quite obscure answers. It might be our school teacher, a lover, or even a friend, but almost without fail the people who have the most important role are those who, if not our natural parents, take on a parental role and direct our take on life. Sometimes these all important people don't hold a place of love and care. They can have the ability to scar our soul and give us a diminished attitude toward love and self-worth. Naturally that can make trust a major issue.

When I hear people say they are committed atheists, I sort of understand and can see how this story, (which I plan to enlarge on) could seem too far-fetched to believe. I do believe though that 'relationship' starts with God and is, in perfect form, all we need to understand about the source of love, and how to find true happiness and peace.

When starting out to discover how they feel about Christianity, lots of people read the Bible beginning with Genesis. Although, if you ask any Christian friend, they will advise you not to start at the beginning, but to look in the Gospels instead. Here we learn far more about God through the life of Jesus. It isn't always easy to understand or believe the story of creation when there are no reference points.

Let us look a little more closely at the significance of the story of the Garden of Eden, the beginning of our relationship with God. In Genesis chapter 1 we're told that God said, "Let us make man in our image, in our likeness." In other words God decided to become the Father of mankind and created a family. Having made Adam, then Eve, God placed them in a garden, which conveys beauty and well-being.

When my husband Roger and I were ready to have a family, we had a similar conversation. We didn't use God's exact words of course, it would be a bit strange if we had said, "Let's have a baby to be like us." Our reason for wanting a child was to extend the love we had for each other, and create another human being to share our life. That is a common reason for having children and I think that's what it is saying in Genesis, although on a much bigger scale!

God as the original Dad, desired to share His life with children who He could love and bring up to know Him and love Him back. Of course, every parent wants to prepare for their children and makes every provision they can for their future, surrounding them with special things. Isn't this what the scripture is saying about God? He provided a place of provision and peace, but also an inheritance, and that's what I want for my children.

We have to remember we are reading about the beginning of time, and so a perfect environment is the picture of the garden. The inheritance was the wonderful world God had created for them to inhabit. Many people do not believe the creation story and see it as a myth. I admit that at first this story can seem unrelated and pretty inconsequential, and would need another book to discuss, but as the concept of relationship and family is the most prominent factor of the text, and indeed the heart of all scripture, it is necessary to start at the beginning. Probably because we have never thought to view God in terms of relationship.

Placing God in the position of a loving and caring father can seem strange. Our 'sophisticated' 21st century mind-set tells us that these things are imaginary. Unfortunately, through the depictions of God in books and films we are likely to form an image of good cop, bad cop. However, in these passages God appears to walk in the garden, a place of beauty. Jesus referred to His Father as the Gardener. I'm sure those who love to garden will appreciate the connection. See John 15:1.

I love to think of Father God walking and enjoying the Garden of Eden. Roger and I have an allotment and as any gardener will tell you it is remarkable how attached you become to every little seed and plant you're cultivating. You care for and protect each one in every way you can to help them develop and thrive.

Good Father, bad Father?

This Father God appears to put a spanner in the works though, by forbidding His children to eat the fruit of the tree of knowledge! I am sure we could argue the case for Adam and Eve's 'human rights', but it seems perfectly logical to me that a parent would warn their child not to touch something they knew would ultimately be bad for them.

In fact, what becomes apparent from all of this is that God had decided to give His children the right to choose. I found allowing my children to make their own decisions really hard sometimes, especially as the things they were warned about most seemed the most attractive. Sadly, Adam and Eve decided to take the advice of the rebellious onlooker depicted in the story as a snake. It certainly did not do Adam and Eve any good disobeying God and eating the forbidden fruit, as Satan would only tempt with things that appear good, but as the Father knew would only bring harm. From this story we know they made their choice, which is an important fact to discover right at the beginning of the scripture, and at the beginning of our discovery into a relationship with a heavenly Father, should we use our right of choice to believe it.

I remember my father telling me not to smoke. He said to me, "I can't stop you, you have to make your own decisions, but you will regret it for years if you make the wrong choice." However, I listened to my friends and took my first cigarette, this led me to smoke for the next twenty years to my great regret.

If you believe the story, why did God do this? Couldn't He just remove whatever was harmful? Well yes of course He could, but a relationship with our children isn't all about dictatorship, even though we need rules.

When we are young and innocent we instinctively trust our parents to lead us, even if we are testing boundaries and our parent's patience, but as we grow older we develop our own ideas and will to follow. We aren't told how old Adam and Eve are obviously old enough to venture out into the realms of self-assertion. Unfortunately for parents, we have to allow our children the freedom to break those rules if they so wish, even when we know it's potentially dangerous. How often have you heard a parent stating mournfully that they would have done anything to prevent their child from making terrible decisions, but who have said in the end "They can only learn from their own mistakes." Do you remember your own? I certainly do.

How it grieves us to see the consequences of the bad choices our children have made. If they had the opportunity, most people would help their children to turn their lives around and start again, without the parent compromising their own stance of course. If we stick with the story we will find that's exactly the position God as our Father decided to take with His children, preferring to trust in His children's love and obedience to do the right thing.

Enter disobedience.

Enter the not so friendly snake, who tempts all of us to throw caution to the wind and take a bite of whatever fruit is available to us, even if we have a voice within saying "Danger!" This is the story of Adam and Eve, and this is also our story.

From then on, even from those familiar Bible stories from our childhood, we can see that Father God comes to the rescue of His children, still begging them to change their ways and bailing them out of desperate situations. He longed for His children to uphold the values He demanded of His family; but they seemed to slip further away.

'My son, do not forget my teaching, but keep my commands in your heart, for they will prolong your life many years and bring you prosperity. Let love and

faithfulness never leave you; bind them around your neck, write them on the tablet of your heart. Then you will win favour and a good name in the sight of God and man. Trust in the Lord with all your heart and lean not on your own understanding; in all your ways acknowledge Him, and He will make your paths straight.' (Proverbs 3:1-6).

When I was at the beginning of my journey of discovery and went to a ladies Bible study, I was that stroppy individual that a leader of any group dreads to encounter, one who tests the resilience of their leadership skills to the utmost. What intrigued me was that through their obedience to the teaching of the Bible and their finding relationship with Jesus, the ladies lives were transformed. As a newcomer, sometimes their decisions seemed naive to me, even ludicrous, but I would be the one with egg on my face when their decisions, based on their belief, brought forth amazing results.

I began to realise this wasn't because of a set of rules or procedures, but from the real loving relationship they had with God the Father and their willingness to trust His wisdom on any matter. But how, I wondered, could that change me? I was to learn just by observation. None of the lovely ladies tried to cajole or convert me, but just growing in understanding in how to love God, and more importantly how He loved me, turned my life around. I was to realize that God interacted with His children through His Word the Bible, and through His Son, Jesus, who came to repair our damaged family.

A break in the family.

Have you heard the saying 'Hate the sin but love the sinner'? Possibly a large percentage of us would know this first hand. For example, people, who through following things that are bad for them, change into someone we don't know any more. They become removed from us because of their behaviour. God did not ban Adam and Eve from eating the fruit in the Garden of Eden just to be a harsh and an unloving father. It was because He knew everything would change and He wouldn't have the same relationship with His children any more. It is significant that all it took was a bite! With that bite, knowledge was unlocked and the power of evil was released. It sounds strong doesn't it? But we all have our own fruit that we are tempted to bite into. If you think about it for instance, one drink or one bet can lead to another and another. One cross word, or one flirtation can lead to something more serious, and like a rolling stone can have devastating consequences if the momentum isn't stopped.

It is said that an over protective mother should break the umbilical cord that is attached to her child, through which she meets their every need. We know the umbilical cord is critical for a child's growth, health and safety while in the womb, but once detached from the nutrients of the mother they can still survive if given the means to be nurtured. This is perhaps a rather obscure description of the separation that occurred when Adam and Eve made the fateful decision to obey Satan and not their Father, God. The connection was severed between them and the essential channel through which their spiritual life was sustained. From then on they would use religion to express their need of God, until they were able to make that connection again. Interestingly, Adam and Eve suddenly became aware of themselves, their nakedness and their wrongdoing. In fear, they hid. We do that don't we? We try to hide the things our conscience tells us are wrong or those things we've been expressively told to do or not do. Of course, like most parents, the Father instinctively knew where they were both in person and in spirit. Just as a mother seems to instinctively know when her child is up to no good in the next room! Then there is a sad sentence in this part of the story as we hear God call to Adam, "Where are you?" To me this is God's heart's cry. As a mother, I have called to my children when they have lost their way. Not literally of course, but in sadness for the child I bore, I've cried as I fail to understand them any more.

God then catches them out - "How do you know you are naked?" They tried to shift the blame, as we all have done at some time or other. But everything had changed, the relationship with their Father was broken and they could not be in His presence. There were reasons for that – their rebellion and disobedience, but more importantly their willingness to listen to the snake, symbolic of Satan, and obey him rather than their Father. In that act they gave someone else the right to shape their thinking and accepted Satan's leading. The world that Father God had given to them as their inheritance, would follow them and become wild and unpredictable. Childbirth, which God had intended to be the joyful extension of His family would be a matter of their own to manage.

The Sad Farewell.

"Yes, I hear you **loud and clear,** but you're old fashioned, out of date."
"Yes, I remember what you said. My friends are here and I am late."
"Yes, I hear you **calling,** but we're all out for fun."
"Perhaps I shouldn't but I don't care, and I am going where you're not there."
"Yes, I hear you **speaking,** but it is plain that you don't know, that this is life and I am grown, and where it takes me I will go."
"Yes, I hear your **whisper**, but it's too late to turn back now, the dye is cast, the choice is made and I can't change it anyhow."
"No! I don't hear your voice, don't say that you have gone!
But I can hear an **echo**."
"**My son, My son, My son.**"

Jill Boyton

FATHER, A GOD OF GRACE.

Fear of God.

It's strange that the thing that religious leaders have used to manipulate their followers is the fear of God. This misunderstanding revolves around relationship, as when you love someone, and that someone is good and kind, you're naturally afraid to hurt or displease them. Not because of any kind of law, but through devotion.

Before I was introduced to this understanding, I shied away from being too involved in anything that smacked of anything less formal than religious observances. I found it frightening to think of being honest about myself to God as I feared His disapproval or anger. We are all aware of at least some of the Ten Commandments, and we all know we can't keep them – not all of them all the time anyway. So what are we to expect of a God that requires that kind of holiness? To my surprise, I found that God's holiness included His grace.

Well, who was He? He was Adam and Eve's Father wasn't He? And He is not going to abandon them or us. He made us, and the love He had for them and us was never in question. The Bible says that their names, and ours, are engraved on His hands. In other words, God's children are never forgotten. There is a saying, 'God doesn't have grandchildren.' Meaning, wherever you are in this journey of life, even if you don't know it, you are a child of God, loved and missed.

'Jesus said, "Suppose one of you had a hundred sheep and loses one of them. Does He not leave the ninety-nine in the open county and go after the lost sheep until he finds it? And when He finds it, he joyfully puts it on his shoulders and goes home. Then he calls his friends and neighbours together and says, 'Rejoice with me; I have found my lost sheep'. I tell you that in the same way there will be more rejoicing in heaven over one sinner who repents than over ninety-nine righteous persons who do not need to repent.'" (Luke 15:3-7).

Roger and I used to run a house as a place for guys to recover from addiction. During that time we came across quite extreme behaviour. We would often be laughed at when we remarked, "He is a good boy really." Not that we thought the behaviour acceptable, but we saw the better part of them and believed that this potential goodness could overcome the things that beset them. In other words, we loved them. They were ours while they lived within the community and we deeply defended the right to care for them. That was not to say there were no rules, or consequences if those rules were broken. I hope even when we weren't conscious of it, we acted with the grace that God always showed us.

God's grace saves the day.

Thankfully, there's a certain amount of safety in laws that tie you down. The responsibility to make the right decisions are made for you, and the right to choose the way you live is taken away. We must have laws to keep us safe, to protect ourselves and others from wrong-doing. The consequences of not having laws is obvious and unfortunately we all know if we didn't have some kind of punishment for breaking them, anarchy would take place. However, that doesn't mean we don't have a free society and have the right to argue our case.

So when God instituted the ten commandments and other laws, He did two things. He set out the guide lines which He wanted His children to adhere to, enabling them to keep to the righteous ways which a Holy God demands, and He entrusted godly men to guide and teach them. If we ask ourselves the question, 'Do we as parents or as a society, make boundaries which we hold sacrosanct so our values are upheld?' Surely our answer would have to be 'yes'. It amuses me that rules we had as parents, that our children would moan about and baulk at, are the very rules they are now applying in their own family life. The most important reason those rules are applied though, are for the well-being of our children. Even though discipline is never received lightly, we know the effect has great benefits for our good. So God as our Father desired for us to have boundaries for our own happiness and well-being.

Trying it the Father's way.

When we have children we try to apply the rules through persuasion. 'No, we don't touch that, do we?' This kind of tactic grows harder though as children develop their own will and their obedience is measured by their desire to do what they're asked. We may not be children, but we obstinately do what we want, if we want to. Amazingly, God, as a loving parent, doesn't abandon us to our own devices, but forgives and restores us through our heartfelt repentance. We'll explore this more in further chapters, but for our explanation of relationship with our Dad, we need to know the heart of God is willing to meet with us when we turn from relying on our own way and the advice of others and turn back to Him for help and direction. Doesn't every parent's heart soar if their rebellious child says, 'I am so sorry Dad, what would you do?'

'My son, do not make light of the Lord's discipline, and do not lose heart when He rebukes you, because the Lord disciplines the ones He loves, and He chastens everyone He accepts as His son.' (Hebrews 12:5,6).

Years ago my husband and I paid our ten pounds and with our young family, packed up our home and belongings and became immigrants to Australia. Moving so far away from our family and friends, not to mention the security we felt in the life we had built up in the U.K. was very frightening. But with the belief that our future could be more rewarding and fulfilled, our excitement and expectation overpowered our fears. However, it was not long before the reality began to hit home, and the fact that wherever you decide to live, life has it's own challenges and problems.

After a while it became apparent that my husband and I wanted different things from this momentous change in our life, and our marriage began to break down. I had some huge decisions to make, which needed wisdom and strength which I couldn't find on my own. I longed for my mother, though she had died sometime before. She knew me - deep down, and was someone who didn't accuse me, but was strong enough in their love to tell me what I didn't want to face, and then stick with me. I knew that my mother would be deeply grieved by the situation and would long to reach out with love and understanding to guide me in what was right. Sadly, so many of us have not experienced that sort of parenting. This causes us to misunderstand the deep cry of the heart of Father God, when He sees the pain of His children and how lost and far from Him they are. This was the Father, although I didn't realize it then, who called out to me "Where are you?"

God was the last person that I would reach out to, how could I turn to Him with such wrong and mixed up circumstances. Like most of us, I believed I couldn't pray or approach God until I was in a better place. It was an amazing fact for me, when first starting out on this journey of Christianity, to discover that I could be 'real' before God, and still be loved, and He just longed to help me. But it was also essential for me to understand, that God loved me before I even knew Him, and He desired to be known and loved by me. Of course, there are many people who don't feel they need to have a relationship with God to be good people, and if you're anything like me you can baulk at the seeming 'Christian' attitude that says otherwise.

However, the truth of the matter is that most of us come to a crisis time in our lives where we evaluate the meaning of who we are and what our lives amount to. We all want to be loved and 'known', possibly in a way that no human, however close, can know us. The truth remains that this life is transient and can change on a sixpence, but the Christian belief is that Father God's love for us goes on for eternity, and when at last we meet Him face to face there will be a wonderful relationship completely restored.

"Are not two sparrows sold for a penny? Yet not one of them will fall to the ground apart from the will of your Father. And even the very hairs of your head are all numbered. So don't be afraid; you are worth more than many sparrows." (Matthew 10:29-31).

A profile of God the Father.

What sort of profile would we give this Father of ours? What clues does the Bible give us? We know He is a God of love, righteousness, peace loving and just, but how about things that bring Him nearer in our understanding of who He is as a person? Here are just a few verses that give us a peep at our Father through fresh eyes.

'If the Lord delights in a man's way, He makes his steps firm; though he stumble, he will not fall, for the Lord upholds him with His hand.' (Psalm 37:23).

Just as we do when we teach our children how to walk or ride a bike.

'The Lord your God is with you, He is mighty to save. He will take great delight in you, He will quiet you with His love, He will rejoice over you with singing.' (Zephaniah 3:17).

Just as we do when we stand with our children as they strive to do the right thing against the pressures of life.

'You are my hiding-place; You will protect me from trouble and surround me with songs of deliverance.' (Psalm 32:7).

Just as we do when we provide a safe place of understanding and love.

'I will signal for them and gather them in. Surely I will redeem them; they will be as numerous as before.' (Zechariah 10:8).

Just as we do when we call and gather our children when we sense danger.

'Do you not know? Have you not heard? The Lord is the everlasting God, the Creator of the ends of the earth. He will not grow tired or weary, and His understanding no-one can fathom. He gives strength to the weary and increases the power of the weak.' (Isaiah 40:28-29).

Just as we do, when vigilant day and night, to provide all our children's needs. So it seems that this Father God is a God of relationship, and longs to show loving kindness, and compassion to those who turn to Him. Just as you and I would love to satisfy our children's needs with good things. I think you'll agree that this is just the sort of heavenly father we all long to have.

Even with all this we are left with questions.

Isn't relationship subjective? How everyone works out their faith is a matter for each individual, isn't it?

Absolutely. Personal understanding is a large part of relationship. For instance, if a child is brought up in a formal and controlled way, much like the former aristocracy brought up their children, then the children would display their affection within the boundaries they were set. The unhappy effect of this could be that neither party would be able to form an 'all embracing' relationship. The Scriptures tell us that whilst retaining His authority and headship, God desires and encourages us to know Him as intimately as we can; within the confines of our human limitations.

The question is though, doesn't this breed familiarity and lack the reverence we should be showing an almighty God?

It's a bit like saying that teachers that allow their pupils to call them by their first names lose their credibility and authority. I quite understand that stance, but a lot of that argument would be based on controlling a group of children. Respect and subsequent control doesn't need to be proved by using a certain name. Relationship and example are the mark of strong leadership. You could argue that the same could be true of our place before God. Who are we to be treating God on the same level as ourselves? But actually what proves to be true is that through Jesus, as we learn and understand who God is, our rightful place before Him, we find His desire is for us to know Him better. As we do this, our respect is the very thing that compels us to worship Him, whilst being allowed to demonstrate our love and praise in a way that bests suits our personality, and circumstances.

When you meet a king or queen shouldn't you treat them with the honour they deserve?

Do they deserve it? Many of the dignitaries that we've been taught to honour have disappointed their followers, leaving them feeling bitter and let down. When Princess Diana, died thousands mourned for her, and there was an outpouring of love towards her. Princess Diana's greatest gift was that she allowed the people of Britain, her expected subjects, to feel she was willing to love and understand them, embracing even those who appeared less acceptable. If we can understand this demographic, couldn't we believe God created us so He could enjoy a more intimate place in our lives. We could say that if we don't accept this argument, God created us for purely egotistic reasons.

I was brought up in an atmosphere of holy reverence, always striving to please the God I loved. I have since learnt though, that humanly I can never fully be all that is considered acceptable, but God loved me first and continues to love me anyway. That fact fills me with such joy that my greatest desire is to know Him more and enable Him to guide and mould me into the person He wants me to be.

What about the commandments?

As you grow closer to God within your relationship, you grow to appreciate His holiness and admire His righteous ways. However, just like a child, this often means learning to obey. The difference is that you know whatever your Father tells you to do is for your own good, and because He loves you.

RELATIONSHIP WITH JESUS

Not for me.

We've spoken of God, Father God, the person we learn of in the Old Testament, but what of the second person in the Godhead, Jesus. He, after all, is who most of us associate with the Bible and the whole God thing. However, Christianity, or the following of Christ, can be scary. Quite often even the mention of 'it' turns you off. I tried to think why that should be. I came to the conclusion that it's all about the idea that God could intrude on our lives. I certainly didn't like the idea of anyone, God, (or even worse any 'good Christian') having a window into my soul, or having an opinion on how I lived my life. I thought that I was doing OK, even though deep down, despite all my best efforts I wasn't coping. We all have times when life overcomes us whether we can identify why or just feel unfulfilled, frightened or disappointed.

Then there were all the big issues. These unfashionable things called sin and forgiveness that Christians had to bring into the mix. It made me feel uncomfortable. Was I really sinful? I was as good as the next person, who needs to do no more than believe that God exists and lives in heaven – wherever that is?

The whole idea of church scared me off. I thought that if I went, people would immediately expect me to join, and then one thing would lead to another, and before I knew what was happening I'd be making commitments I didn't want to make. There were also the really boring things that could interfere in your life – time spent thinking of 'God'. The new people it involved, not really my type! It all seemed really complicated, best to leave it alone. I for one had more on my mind than this. I tried hard at being detached from it all. But something strange happened. Deep down I was being evermore drawn to the whole 'faith' thing, but I didn't know why. I felt really exposed and yet I wanted to dabble in the knowledge of God. Perhaps you feel the same sometimes?

Is anybody there?

I imagine that most people, even the most anti-God types, turn to prayer when they or their loved ones are in trouble. For a minute they want to believe there is a higher power greater than themselves that can make a difference. When I was in Australia I was dragged along by my friend to a neighbour's Bible study group. Not only did I feel out of place, but I felt embarrassed, for myself and them. With their singing and praying, I didn't think they were in touch with the real world. You probably think what a wild statement, but it's what I thought at the time. I was a new immigrant. Roger and I had mortgaged ourselves up to the hilt to buy a house, working opposite shifts to pay it off. Having three children at the time, we were always broke and tired. My first reaction was that these ladies were well placed, well meaning, way out Christians who knew little of how the real world worked. How wrong I was, as after a week or two I realised their lives were no different to mine, yet they were infinitely different because of their faith.

Relationship.

I was not an easy member of the group. I was always trying to come up with arguments which proved my knowledge and credibility. Each week as I left I vowed I would never go back. The love and friendship of each of the ladies was so special, but I was much too afraid to allow them close to me. The strange thing was, they always accepted me and despite myself I always went back.

Jesus knows.

Most of my feelings of discomfort came from the knowledge that I hadn't lived in a way that was in keeping with Christian belief. Every week we'd look at a chapter of a gospel and discuss it. I was amazed how normal, yet supernatural, it all was. Their prayers for their families and friends (and I'm sure I was secretly included), were answered. Their most difficult situations were given a new hope and faith that God was very much involved. Of course, I tried hard to hide the real me. I'd pretend I knew just as much as they did. I'd argue any point which might challenge me or expose the fact I really didn't feel I could fit into this good Jesus loving life.

The door swings wide.

Do you remember the part in 'The Lion, The Witch, and the Wardrobe' that describes the entrance into Narnia, that strange and mystical land? It certainly felt like that to me on the day everything changed. Like the children in the story, I too was hiding among the coats in the back of my own metaphorical wardrobe, not wanting to be found. Suddenly though, all my sins, my selfish life, my wrongdoings came flooding over me. Almost without even knowing it, I was on my knees before my friends. They hadn't influenced me to do this, but all at once Jesus was real and accepting me, even though the things I had thought and done needed God's forgiveness. The reality of the payment Jesus made through His death for my sins became overwhelming, and in that moment the door swung wide and I fell into my Narnia – the arms of Christ.

Truth revealed.

Even writing down these events brings tears to my eyes. Yet knowing I had to have a change of heart before I came to know the same truth that my friends had known and shown to me. Each person has their own special journey and encounter with Jesus. He remains unique for each of us. For me the best description is the experience we've all felt at least once – falling in love. We could all explain our deep and real feelings and yet it is our own precious encounter.

The reason.

I will forever be in the debt of my dear friends who, though faced with an argumentative candidate, modelled the nature of Christianity and left it to

Jesus to cause me to fall in love with Him. Now my desire is to do the same. To bring forward in an explanation the relational heart of Christianity, so hopefully others like me can be introduced to this amazing person.

Jesus who?

Things changed for me when I really began to appreciate who Jesus is and how I relate to Him. When we meet people for the first time we look at their appearance, but then quite quickly we make an assessment on who we think they are by their behaviour. We then begin to fill in the gaps by finding out more about their background. It is only then that we decide whether we could develop a relationship with them, or not as the case might be. As we meet up with Jesus in this chapter, it's important to keep this in mind. You may be surprised by some of the answers and the kind of relationship Jesus could possibly want to have with us.

Don't judge a book by its cover.

When I was young I was brought up in a Roman Catholic household. To me Jesus was the man I saw in the statues and stained glass windows of my church. We didn't study the Bible and the Mass was all in Latin, which meant my knowledge of Jesus started with the Christmas story and ended with the cross. However, through my visits to the ladies Bible study group, I began to look past my impressions of Jesus with pale skin and dressed in gleaming white who seemingly hovered above the ground, to someone who walked a lot, probably had very dirty feet and clothes and mixed with a suspect group of people. I wonder what impression you have of Jesus from all you've gleaned from the information available to you?

Also the facts my friends found in the scriptures and pointed out to me, seemed to portray a different kind of man to the one I had imagined. As he'd been a carpenter's son, a workman and not a stranger to hard work. He probably hit his thumb, haggled over prices and paid heavy taxes. He was also the eldest son, and having not started his ministry until he was thirty, had taken the major responsibility for his family. The scriptures don't mention Joseph, his earthly father, after Jesus' twelfth birthday. It's presumed that sometime between then and the crucifixion, Joseph had died. Also I learnt that Jesus' home town of Nazareth didn't have a great reputation either. Nathaniel, a disciple of Jesus, when being told about Him for the first time said, - "Does anything good come out of Nazareth?"

Not only was Jesus born in a stable instead of a palace, his family were forced to flee from Israel to Egypt, so were refugees. Then at the time, a tyrant called Herod the Great, had heard of his birth through prophesy which had been given in the old Jewish scriptures, that a great king would be born at this time. Herod saw this as a threat to his reign and so ordered all male children below the age of two to be killed, a fact which is well documented. Nazareth wasn't a backwater. It was a major trade route and encompassed a Roman garrison. We tend to forget that Israel was an occupied country, which as well as bringing a multicultural community, must have brought all sorts of resentments and difficulties. Jesus would have been well aware of the tensions, hardships and political injustice. Jesus was very spiritual and would have been well versed in the Torah - the Jewish scripture that makes up some of the Old Testament today. Once while visiting Jerusalem, He had been found by his mother and father in the temple teaching the priests by explaining the scriptures. He was around twelve at the time. It seemed He was learning who He really was, and who His real Father was too. This was the young Jesus, son of God, son of Man.

But why was He here?

At the beginning of His ministry, Jesus made a name for himself at a wedding in Cana. Miraculously, He turned water into wine, saving the day for the host who had seriously under estimated the amount of wine his guests would drink. Sound familiar? It was his mother's idea that he should intervene and Mary's faith that encouraged him to perform his first miracle. It was an act which showed kindness and understanding, but more than that, it also showed Jesus was passionate about the message of redemption His Father had entrusted to him to give.

This social event marked the beginning of the interaction between the ordinary and the divine. It was clear that men couldn't deal with the things in their human nature which led them to sin. Sin being those things which we do, think or say which miss the mark in regards to being good. This meant that God's children were separated from His righteousness and the blessings that were rightfully theirs. The Jewish nation had a special mission, to live as God's children, obeying His commandments, loving God and each other. Sadly, even when devout and godly men tried to turn them back to God, they chose to live without Him.

Jesus came not as a prophet, not even as a worldly king, but as God's Son, living as a man. He was completely human, but being conceived in Mary's womb by the Holy Spirit, He was God, living with the same propensity as man. He could be tempted and hurt, feel happy and sad, and could certainly love and be loved. But that was beyond anything we could imagine – the unconditional love of God. It was for this purpose Jesus came to show all mankind the real nature of the Godhead and redeem those who had been lied to. It was clear He was self-effacing humble and real. He didn't take people at face value, but understood their weaknesses and worked with them.

There's a saying used about Christians sometimes that says: 'He is so heavenly minded he is no earthly good'. This certainly isn't true of Jesus as no one, then or now, has been unable to approach this lovely person and not feel that He understands exactly where they're coming from. He is aware of the things that tempt us because God allowed Him to be tempted. He knows the physical pain of the cross, the pain of rejection and misunderstanding. He can perfectly judge our motivations.

'The teachers of the law and the Pharisees brought in a woman caught in adultery. They made her stand before the group and said to Jesus, "Teacher, this woman was caught in the act of adultery. In the Law, Moses commanded us to stone such women. Now what do you say?" They were using this question as a trap, in order to have a basis for accusing Him. But Jesus bent down and started to write on the ground with His finger. When they kept on questioning Him, He straightened up and said to them, "If any one of you is without sin, let him be the first to throw a stone at her." Again He stooped down and wrote on the ground. At this, those who heard began to go away one at a time, the older ones first, until only Jesus was left, with the woman still standing there. Jesus straightened up and asked her, "Woman where are they? Has no-one condemned you?" "No-one, sir," she said. "Then neither do I condemn you," Jesus declared, "Go now and leave your life of sin."' (John 8:3-11).

Can you imagine the attitudes of the people in Nazareth when they were told that Joseph wasn't Jesus' father, but God Himself. How would His siblings perceive their half brother? We can have enough difficulty explaining our family situations! This reputation followed Jesus and added to the way in which the establishment saw His love and care as an insult to their religion. All of this didn't exactly make it an easy life for the most special person who ever set foot on earth. But what it did produce was a person who actually lived with the kind of trials we ourselves suffer, and made Him a friend we know we can trust. For me, learning that was so reassuring.

Son of God, Son of Man.

In both Matthew's and Luke's gospels the genealogy of Jesus is recorded. Matthew's account gives the birth line from Abraham to Joseph, ending:- *'Joseph husband of Mary, by whom was born Jesus, who is called the Christ'* (Matthew 1:1-17). However, Luke uses a slightly different approach. Luke starts from the opposite end by citing the ministry of Jesus first and questions the father of Jesus by saying *'Supposedly' the son of Joseph'*. Then listing from Joseph, he prefixes each name entered with 'Son of ....' until reaching Adam and calling Him the 'Son of God.' Luke 3:23-38. Jesus gave Himself the title, 'Son of Man' and here Luke links the humanity of Jesus to the divine. Frequently in the gospels, 'Son of God' and 'Son of Man' interlink, and more often that not it is Jesus being quoted. So what can we make of this in our profiling of Jesus and how it can make a difference to our relationship. To do this we need to revisit the Garden of Eden and the origins that Luke mentioned. We need to take into consideration that the Son of God living as the Son of Man, lays down His kingship and lives a life we wouldn't find easy.

'As they were travelling along the road someone said to Him, "I will follow you wherever you go." Jesus told him, "The foxes have holes, and birds have nests, but the Son of Man does not have a place to lay His head."' (Luke 9:57-58).

Truth revealed.

Christians believe that all three members of the Holy Trinity, the Godhead, were present and part of the creation. It is recorded that God said: "Let Us make man in Our image, according to Our likeness." Adam was intended to have the nature of God, to be like Him and this to be handed down from generation to generation. They were to fill the earth with love and light, joy and peace. It's a great thought. No more worrying about bad things happening. Being able to bring our children up in safety, with a hope for the future. In effect our genealogy would also go back to God the Father. You'll remember that like Adam and Eve our nature allows us to make our own choices, which can lead us to be deceived and to reject our parentage. God gave us the right to do this, but who would want to?

Jesus called Satan the father of all lies; he still is. Does this all seem a bit far fetched? Well you would think so, until you consider the choices you've made that seemed good at the time, but turned out to trap you and maybe even make you do things you really didn't want to do. We could carry on down this track, but you get the picture don't you?

The love of the Father.

I love to spend time with a certain friend of mine Jim, who has a young family. His parenting skills are second to none and remind me of how our relationship with our heavenly Father should be. Jim is often found sitting on the sofa, sometimes under a duvet, watching cartoons with his children, or out with them cycling, playing football or swimming. However, what Dad says is expected to be obeyed. Bed-time is bed-time and little chores have to be done. Of course the children complain and show-off at times, but hard though it is they're disciplined in an appropriate way. When the due time has elapsed and apologies are made, kisses and cuddles restore the harmony and love.

We can have a loving father who's love is also combined with respect and obedience. God doesn't reign through terror, but He also doesn't tolerate those things that compromise His values. So if Jesus was to come against the legalistic religious lies, to reveal Father God as He truly is, He too would have to come as a man. He would be like us, He could be hurt, cold, weary. He could be misunderstood and sad. Jesus could also have a great sense of humour, be a great friend, compassionate and loving. He is of course, just like His Dad. If you like Him, you'll love His Dad. Is that a bit disrespectful? Well Jesus did tell us when we pray to address our Father in a more loving and intimate way, using the Aramaic word 'Abba', which means Daddy. I think it makes a difference, feeling that our heavenly Father can say of us, as He definitely did of Jesus, "That's My boy or girl" which ever the case might be.

JESUS THE REDEEMER.

Son of God.

When Jesus was baptised He was making a public declaration which said: I know who I am, and the reason I am here, and I am committed to my Father and the task before me. God the Father responded. He audibly spoke. *"You are My Son whom I love; with you I am well pleased."* (Mark 1:11).

At this, the scripture says the third member of the Trinity appeared as a dove. His presence signifying God's anointing. The gloves were off, Jesus had started the task for which He was called, to take back that which had been stolen – us.

Directly after His baptism Jesus was lead by the Holy Spirit to be tested, just as Adam and Eve had been, by Satan. After forty days of fasting in the desert Satan turns up again and began his deceiving tactics. He uses the same argument on us very successfully, especially when we're at our weakest. But this was Jesus as a man and just as vulnerable. His strength would lie in His knowledge of God the Father and His Word.

The Devil playing on His hunger and physical need gave the first test: "*If you are the Son of God, tell this stone to become bread.*" Jesus answered by quoting Deuteronomy: "*It is written: 'Man does not live on bread alone.'*" He was saying that it takes more than bread to really live. God's Word was, and is called the 'Bread of Life.' Spreading out the kingdoms of the earth, the Devil lead Him up to a high place and showed Him in an instant all the kingdoms of the world. He said to Jesus, "I will give you all their authority and splendour, for it has been given to me, and I can give it to anyone I want to. So if you worship me, it will all be yours." His second temptation was the desire for power and possession. Jesus answered, ' It is written: 'Worship the Lord your God and serve Him only.'

The devil led Him to Jerusalem and had Him stand on the highest point of the temple. "If you are the son of God," he said, "throw yourself down from here. For it is written: 'He will command His angels concerning you to guard you carefully; They will lift you up in their hands, so that you will not strike your foot against a stone.'" Jesus answered "It says; Do not put the Lord your God to the test." These passages are taken from Luke 4:3-12 & Matt 4:1-11.

In short, Satan tried to make Jesus believe and do what he said, instead of listening and doing what His Father told Him. He tried to make Him believe that if He did what Satan told Him He would be better than God. However, unlike Adam and Eve, Jesus stood firm and Satan left Him for a time. Jesus had been obedient and fulfilled His title 'Son of God' by being like God in all His ways. What an ordeal. Jesus, weakened in the body and battered in spirit, needed the angels who came to minister to Him, but He prevailed and had started on His amazing journey.

Jesus the man.

Having found the heritage of Jesus and His family history, we catch up with Him through the gospels. At around the age of thirty Jesus began His teaching. The name for teacher was Rabbi and there were many of them, travelling around expounding on the scriptures and gathering their own followers. So it was not the fact that Jesus was teaching which was different, it was what He was teaching, how He was teaching and most importantly what He was doing! Not only was Jesus divine and human, His teaching was ordinary, yet spiritual. He used agriculture, relationship and ordinary things that everyone would know as the basis for His preaching. He spoke in the open so that anyone could leave when they wanted to, and everyone knew and understood where He was coming from. Or did they?

Jesus is amazingly clever, the stories and issues He spoke on could mean totally different things to those who heard. He had the ability to speak to a crowd and yet make each individual feel as though He saw directly into their soul, and spoke just to them. Does that feel a bit spooky? Well if someone spoke truth into your heart, situation or purpose, you'd feel a bit freaked out wouldn't you? But if that person revealed the answer, with love and understanding you'd sit up, listen and run back to tell your friends. Not only that, Jesus started talking about God as though He knew Him intimately. This was a huge 'no no' as far as the Jewish religious establishment was concerned. They weren't allowed to even speak the name of God. Yet Jesus encouraged His followers to address Him in a much more affectionate way - 'Abba father' meaning Daddy. But by using this seemingly innocuous word meant the death penalty under the religious laws at the time.

Not long after Roger and I had become Christians we met by chance a young Pastor and his wife. The guy looked like an Aussie workman with his rolled up shorts and his working boots, a real Ocker. He and his wife had just taken up a job with another minister called John Smith. John, the son of a Methodist minister, had decided to turn his back on conventional church and from a call he felt from God, reach out to those least likely to attend a church service, prostitute's and Hell's Angels bikers! The story of John Smith's journey is well known, but to Roger and I it was all new. We decided to visit their church, which, as our new friend told us, was built by the congregation from mud bricks. When we arrived the long building was surrounded by chopper bikes, one of which was John's. We didn't have to worry if we were late for the start, as the service went on all day. Just as Jesus had spoken on a hill to people who were free to come and go as they wished, so John's church services were designed to have the same freedom.

Inside, the seating was from an old cinema and instead of an altar, a huge fire place took centre stage. The music was played on any instrument that was available, including a banjo and harmonica! Trying to ignore the smell of cigarette smoke which wafted from the back of the room, our family relaxed in this radical but unconditional atmosphere. Here was an opportunity for those attending not to be compromised in their ability to listen to the words of Jesus by the so call protocol of church. They were free to feel that they were understood and respected by the people who represented Jesus. This was the character that Jesus displayed, embracing all who wished to listen and learn from Him, added to which He was performing amazing miracles.

Jesus loved the people, often those who were the least loved, and they loved Him right back. He loves us too and His message is for us just as much as those He met in Israel. But the scribes, teachers, Sadducees and priests, hated Him. Today He has just as many enemies. He knows all this, but He doesn't let their opposition deter Him. He was there to bring a message and give it in such a way that those who heard Him knew it was beyond insightful. It was 'relational' because it reflected the love of a Father.

The way of the cross.

As a girl I used to walk around the 'stations of the cross,' in our church during Lent. 'Stations of the cross' are pictures depicting the passion of Christ as He went to the cross. I spent a long time thinking about how this journey of suffering would have been for Jesus. So we are going to take a much closer look at what the cross means to Christians. But for our profiling of Jesus and His relationship with us in the family of God, we're going to examine what brought Him this far.

In times past, many had been sent to the Jewish nation. Prophets were righteous men called by God to tell the people to repair all that had been undone in their relationship with Him by continuing to be disobedient and sinful. Mostly these servants of the Lord were scorned, imprisoned, or killed. As we've discussed, the Israelites were doing much as they wanted to do and talk of obedience was a message which fell on deaf ears. The Israelites didn't want to follow a set of rules which supposedly made them more righteous and closer to God. Does that sound familiar? Of course there were times when there were real difficulties and they would turn back to God and ask to be forgiven. He heard them when they cried out to Him and rescued them, but it was short lived. They soon went back to living with at best some kind of religion, and at worst not having any kind of contact with God at all.

Then into the same arena Jesus came, but this time not as the servant, but as the master. It was the same message, this time out of the mouth of the Son of God, but there was something different. There was no compromise in dealing with the sin that prevented their union with their Father. In fact, Jesus spelt out in detail that sin was the catalyst for disaster as far as a relationship with God was concerned. So what was the difference?

Jesus came with the love of the Father. He said He had not come to condemn the world, but to save it. He wept for those who turned away from God and snubbed the hand their Father was holding out to them. What could bridge the gap? How could the unrighteousness be paid for and God's children be restored?

The mandate.

Jesus returned to Nazareth where He was raised and as He always did on a Sabbath, He went to the

Synagogue. When He stood up to read, He was handed the scroll of the prophet Isaiah. Unrolling the scroll, He read:

'The Spirit of the Lord is on Me, because He has anointed me to preach good news to the poor. He has sent me to proclaim freedom for the prisoners and recovery of sight for the blind, to release the oppressed, to proclaim the year of the Lords favour.' (Luke 4:16-19).

There is a story that explains the concept of redemption.

A beautiful silver jar had been stolen from its owner. It had been made to hold precious oil, but before it could be used it had been stolen. So priceless was the jar that the owner sent many to find it, until at last it was found, not by the servants but by the son of the owner. However, its beauty had been marred by misuse and it was tarnished and battered. Nevertheless, the son recognised its worth. The price that was asked to redeem the jar was great, but the son was willing to give all that He owned to buy it back. Once the jar had been purchased He gently cleaned it and restored it and presented it to His Father with great joy, for it to be filled with oil for the healing of the nations.

Sadly the Jewish leaders didn't want to be found or redeemed, they didn't want the people to disregard their previous attitudes to God. So like the servants before, they killed the messenger.

Lover of our souls.

I love those words – 'Lover of our souls.' Never had someone willingly and without obvious reason given everything in love for mankind. During His last days Jesus endured His greatest trial. He, like us, had free will. However unlike us, He had the power to change His destiny. Although, He suffered agony of soul before His Father, asking if there was another way, knowing that the scriptures told of His whipping with a cat of nine tails, His willingness was never in question.

He was beaten until He became unrecognisable, His beard pulled out and a crown made of long thorn briar's pierced His head. Nevertheless, He was willingly led to His suffering and death. Stripped of dignity, His hands nailed out as though to connect the two loves of His soul – His Father God and us. Each one of us. Knowing us, understanding us, He cried out, "*Father forgive them, they know not what they do."* He suffered the worst death of a common criminal, with a sign that called Him 'King of the Jews' nailed above His head. But we're familiar with this figure of Christ, even wearing His instrument of execution around our necks. What we may not be familiar with is the real reason for this horror. Our God, taunted and jeered at, took this suffering punishment for each one of us. As His garments were stripped from Him, so too were our sins. All our evil thoughts and deeds, even those that no-one knows of, were stripped from us and laid on Him to be paid for as a common criminal.

The most desperate moment came when Jesus became sin and His Father couldn't receive Him. In that moment He cried out to His Father, for Himself but also for us, "*My God, My God, why have you forsaken me?*" Have you ever cried out to God like that? If you have, you now know you're in good company.

As Jesus died, our sins, those things that make us unacceptable to God, died with Him. We were made clean through His death. The price for our sin was paid in full by Jesus. This is the love of God, giving His only son to die for our sins so that we can be reunited. Not only loving those who love

Him back, but also those who despise Him. We need only to confess our sins and unrighteousness to receive His everlasting love and relationship. In other words God worked out a way that we can choose to be His again! What a man. What a God. What a Father. Lover of our souls.

You'll know that to Christians Easter Sunday is special because this is when we celebrate the resurrection of Jesus. Still bearing the scars of the crucifixion, Jesus rose three days after His death and appeared to the disciples. This was the final sign of His place in the Holy Trinity as the Son of God and also confirmation of our place with Him in eternity. As Jesus died, but lives, so do we. Our comfort is that this life is the beginning of a life even more wonderful than we could ever imagine, and all this through the love of God and the obedience of Jesus.

What's this to me?

Having given some idea of who Jesus really is, what now? Why does any of this have any bearing on our lives? The clue is in the chapter title – Jesus the Redeemer. Let me explain. I wonder what would have happened if we had lived and been around when Jesus walked the land of Israel? If our friend had come and said, "*Hey that guy Jesus from Nazareth is speaking down by the lake today. I'm going, are you?*" I wonder what our response would be. Would we go and sit far at the back so we could not be seen, or would we push to the front so we didn't miss a word? When we had been listening all day and we were hungry, would we moan and groan or would we stay on, eating the bread that Jesus miraculously supplied for those who stayed to the end? I wanted to say, "Yes! I want to stay. Don't forget me!" He never has forgotten.

The mission of Jesus was to reveal God's love for us, whether we're sitting in a mud brick hall, or in an open field, in someone's sitting room or in a conventional church. He gives to us the chance to make a decision, to wash away the wrong that has been done originally. Not only that, but also to be reunited to our Father, individually and corporately so that no one need be destroyed. By believing in Him, anyone can have a whole and lasting life. God didn't go to all the trouble of sending His Son merely to point an accusing finger, telling the world how bad it was. He came to help, to put the world right again. Read John 3:16-17.

We have established that Jesus came to redeem you and me, buy us back, bring us home, love us and give us the right to love Him right back. Who wouldn't want to have a relationship like this? But do we? I guess we have to ask ourselves what makes a relationship, and where does Jesus fit into what we'd expect? There are all sorts of relationships as we know, and each of them has an expected attitude or behaviour. We've spoken of the place of a father and more especially our Father God, but what do we expect of Jesus? There are three roles particularly close to us. One, is the role of a spouse, another is a 'brother' (sister), and lastly a friend. All of these people have a special ability to interact with us in an intimate and understanding way. Jesus indicated that these are the special roles He plays in our relationship with God.

For instance, even with the special connection we have with our father, mother and children, we would not tell them, the things we might share with our friend, brother or spouse. With our partners we have an intimacy that we don't have with any other being. They are our soul-mate and often the father or mother of our children. It's more likely that our husbands or wives are the ones we rant at, knowing they won't love us any less. They're the only person who truly knows all the ups and downs of our family life and with whom we are 'up close and personal.'

A brother knows us from way back when, they understand some of the history of how we tick. The experience of their childhood is the same as ours and hopefully we can have a special camaraderie. 'Blood is thicker than water' the saying goes, and we should know that when the chips are down, our sibling will stick with us.

Then there is the friend. A friend walks with us, throws away the bad bits and keeps what is good. Someone who cries at films with us, shouts at football matches with us, banters with us and sticks up for us when we need it. A friend is there at the end of a phone with advice and a shoulder to cry on, keeps good counsel and forgives us when they need not do so. You may say, "I don't have any relationships like that." I am sorry if you don't. Jesus is always ready to share in our lives in that personal way when we give Him the chance.

THE COMPELLING PERSON OF JESUS.

Peace is the overwhelming quality and power that attracts me to Jesus. He has a sense of His own assurance and peace within Himself, giving Him an ability to accept others without prejudice, but imparting love and wisdom, if you're to listen and understand. Kindness, patience and compassion, make Him totally approachable. Most of all, a love that does not depend on anything more than our existence.

Sadness and sorrow give a depth to Jesus, that is unique and profound. Observing the destructive powers at work in our lives, that snatch the peace and joy that is rightfully ours can move Him to tears and ultimately to death. Yet celebration and joy overrides all this and gives to Jesus a vibrancy that joins Him to everything about this universe that is good and worthy of praise. Who could not be compelled to fall at the feet of such a man, such a friend, lover and saviour? Who could not want to worship a creator who embraces us in such a wonderful all-encompassing way and be grateful to call Him Lord.

Even with all of this we are left with questions.

Christians talk about Jesus being like a friend, but how can He be when bad things happen even when you pray that they won't?

This question is often asked, and it's obviously difficult to answer when there are so many who don't appear to have the answers to their prayers. It's clear that not all the world wants to believe and follow Jesus. One day this world will have reached its final destiny, everyone will have had their opportunity to believe in redemption through the cross. Until then though, both Christians and non Christians are subject to the bad things that happen. Sometimes we see healing. Sometimes Jesus walks through our pain with us and makes something wonderful of the adversity that we suffer. Just as He did on the cross. All who come to God in faith see an answer to their prayer, many not immediately, and maybe not in the way they expected. However, God does answer prayer and honours faith, often in ways that are profound.

If Jesus didn't come to condemn, why can't He save everyone?

He can. The only proviso is that we really want to be saved. We have our own will and it's up to us. If we tell God that we repent of those things we've done wrong, we believe in Jesus and the fact He died on the cross for our sins. We finally want to follow Him always.

Does Jesus hear our prayers even if we aren't Christians?

Definitely, God loves us to pray. Prayer is just speaking to God. He'll do everything to help you to know Him more intimately, but it does depend on your willingness.

RELATIONSHIP WITH THE HOLY SPIRIT

The Helper.

When we first start exploring the realms of Christianity it's almost inevitable that our sense of reason locks horns with what we feel is completely unreasonable. I believe that God was good to me, as I had embraced the message of the gospel and decided to become a committed Christian before being confronted with the third person of the Holy Trinity. If the question of accepting the reality of the Holy Spirit had been brought up at the beginning, I would have backed off and missed out on knowing my wonderful Father God and my Saviour Jesus.

My introduction to the Holy Spirit was quite bizarre and happened as I cleaned the walls of the operating theatre and swept up all the bits of gut left by the surgeon as he sewed up his patient. I'd like to tell you I was a theatre nurse, or even something grander, but the truth is I was just a night cleaner in the 'bush' hospital, delegated to clean the theatre. However, God works in wondrous ways and it was there I formed a friendship with the real theatre nurse, who sterilised the instruments and laid them out for the next day. Like me, she was an immigrant to Australia. She was a Yorkshire girl and hadn't lost her straight talking approach. We would both gown up and her big brown eyes stared out under her dark green theatre scarf, making her quite a formidable character. It wasn't long before she was talking to me about her Christian faith and in particular the Holy Spirit. To be honest, her 'no messing' approach frightened me to bits and just the sound of the 'Holy Spirit' seemed dodgy. 'Was she a member of a cult?' I kept my distance and wasn't won over by her explanations.

When I left that job she presented me with a small book which pointed out the passages in the Bible where the Holy Spirit was mentioned and an explanation of how and why Christians need Him in their lives. Much later Roger and I read this together, which led us to accepting and receiving the Holy Spirit, and asking Him into our lives. Just as we had done with Jesus. However, no one explained to us in simple language the place the Holy Spirit holds within the Holy Trinity, or how important His role is in our personal journey and the role of the church. Therefore, it is important we grasp the need we have of the help of this third and equally great member of the Holy Trinity. To that end, I hope I can explain the place of the Holy Spirit.

What's in a name?

The first place to go when answering this question is, what do we understand 'spirit' to mean. We use it in many different ways - 'the spirit of the age', 'the spirit of fair play', 'very spirited', 'brave spirit', etc. All these terms explain the person, or their heart, and what the essence of their personality is. The Bible shows what is meant by Spirit by the many ways in which we see His personality or work. Jesus put it like this, *"The wind blows wherever it pleases. You hear its sound, but you cannot tell where it comes from or where it is going."* (John 3:8).

Of late, we have a graphic example in our wind farms. For years we've used the wind to serve us, whether in transportation, energy, fertilisation, or production, the source of the wind has served us well. So could the Spirit of God be the essence of God? The person of God? Jesus spoke of Him in a relational way, *"I will send Him to you"* and *"When He comes"* (John 16:7-8).

Jesus also said the Holy Spirit would only say and do what He, Jesus, wanted Him to. Jesus had also done the same and only acted and said what He knew the Father instructed.

So here we have three different people all of one mind and personality. There is a great passage which says, 'A *cord of three strands is not quickly broken.*' (*Ecclesiastes 4:12*). Three strands are used in every rope. Its strength comes from the fact that they are bound together. The tighter they are pulled the stronger they become. Each strand is individual in itself, but put together there's no division between them and they make one rope.

We see Jesus, we hear the Father's voice, but we know the Holy Spirit by 'who' He is, and what He 'does' in us and for others. So let's follow that through. If Jesus is like His Father, and the Holy Spirit is like Jesus, and Holy Spirit is interacting with us, does that mean that we could be in the family of God?

'"You should not be surprised at my saying, 'You must be born again.' The wind blows wherever it pleases. You hear its sound, but you cannot tell where it comes from or where it's going. So it is with everyone born of the Spirit."' (John 3:7-8).

The spirit in the bottle is the most obvious one we missed out, but how could we use that as an example of God? Well there is a sort of obscure comparison. If you have a bottle of whisky it might have a good name, you could buy the most expensive, have the best recommendation, but only when you tasted it would you really prove its worth. Likewise with the wind turbines, they might be a wonderful feat of engineering but they're only effective with the 'spirit' of the wind.

What's in a title?

Well we all have titles – Mr, Mrs etc. Our status sets out where we stand in relation to everyone else. Jesus doesn't just use the word 'spirit' in His introduction, but gives Him His title, 'Holy' Spirit. I looked the word 'holy' up in the thesaurus and it said things like, sacred, consecrated, hallowed, divine. Of course they're all right, but I like the explanation given in the Bible where the nature of the Holy Spirit is explained in terms of what His presence brings forth.

'Love, joy, peace, patience, kindness, and goodness. Faithfulness, gentleness, and self control.' (Galatians 5:22-23).

I love this particular explanation I found in a Bible commentary which shows the essence of all three of the God-head – LOVE.

Joy is love's strength.
Peace is love's security.
Patience is love's endurance.
Kindness is love's conduct.
Goodness is love's character.
Gentleness love's humility.
Self-control love's victory.

I would say that says Holiness wouldn't you? Of course to be holy is no mean feat, and I would presume no Christian would dare to say so. However, the Holy Spirit works with us, changing our thinking, pointing out those things we never gave a thought to, as being unholy. The more we spend time reading the Bible and in prayer, the more the Holy Spirit changes our desires almost without us realising it. Of course God never takes away our right to choose, and so quite often we have to call on the Holy Spirit to change our thinking to do the right thing. Often there are hard choices, painful and difficult. As Jesus taught us to, turn the other cheek, walk the extra mile, forgive when injured. Sometimes those actions which seem small and insignificant in the main have to be addressed, and not only those things we do, but those we don't do. All these things the Holy Spirit helps us with.

We have, as we have explained, been brought into the family of God. Saint Paul puts it like this, *'Because those who are led by the Spirit of God are sons of God. For you did not receive a spirit that makes you a slave again to fear, but you received the Spirit of sonship. And by Him we cry 'Abba Father.' The Spirit Himself testifies with our spirit that we are God's children.'* (Romans 8:14-16).

The things of greatest importance to us usually revolve around relational things - our self worth, family life, love life and how we cope etc. These things can be improved or damaged by those who have the most to do with us. God is good at relationship, I hope we've covered that fact. The Bible tells us that the Holy Spirit is 'the Comforter' and 'the Guide.' He helps us to discern how we should proceed, gives us wisdom and teaches us about ourselves and others. He only works for the common good, reminds us about the things that Jesus says and who our Father wants us to be. He opens up our mind to the Word of God which is the Bible, brings life and nurtures us. There is so much more the Holy Spirit does, but it would have to be a very big book to tell you all He achieves if we let Him.

Unconditional love does have a condition!

Although Jesus assures us and wishes all of us to know and receive the love and help of the Holy Spirit, He can be grieved away from us.

Jesus told the disciples that He had to leave them so that the Holy Spirit could come. Why couldn't the Holy Spirit come while Jesus was alive if He was part of the God-head? Well the clue is in the name again. The Holy Spirit had never before come in the same way to the people of God, He had always been there, interacting with those who believed in Him, but this time it was different. This time He would live in those who believed in Jesus. All those attributes we've spoken of would be theirs if they lived their life in harmony with Him. However, this was only possible because Jesus had died, and through His death our sins were forgiven. We could be a Holy place, a temple, in which God's Spirit can live.

You might quite rightly say, "I don't see all the Christians I know being that holy." Well no, and when we sin it prevents us from fully giving glory to God, which is the main task of the Holy Spirit, as it was for Jesus. As Jesus died that we might be forgiven, the Holy Spirit convicts us of those things that aren't right, so that we can ask for forgiveness and turn back to being in harmony with God again. When we refuse to repent, we prevent the Holy Spirit from living through us to the extent that a righteous God desires, and so we grieve Him. As I am writing this it seems quite legalistic, but of course it's the situation we're familiar with in our close relationships. For instance, when our children are disobedient, the relationship changes. We still love them, but they're not acting in a way that's good, so they make it hard for us to continue in harmony until they've made amends and admitted their wrong-doing. When parents allow their children to act badly it reflects on them, in the same way our sin can't be allowed to reflect on God's good character. So for that time the Holy Spirit detaches Himself from us. However, He doesn't desert us, but encourages us to find our way back to our Father to seek forgiveness and be restored.

'In the same way, the Spirit helps us in our weakness. We do not know what we ought to pray for, but the Spirit himself intercedes for us with groans that words cannot express. And He who searches our hearts knows the mind of the Spirit, because the Spirit intercedes for us in accordance with God's will.' (Romans 8:26-27).

Knowing and receiving the Holy Spirit.

God is shrewd, He knows how to cut His cloth. We're now in the family business and He'll use each of us according to who we are. Those who have accepted Jesus are now His co-workers and our purpose is to tell others the Good News about who we really are and how our Father gave His only Son that everyone should once again be restored to His family. This is called our great commission. In those first years of knowing the Holy Spirit, I was still pretty unaware of this person and all He brought. I knew the love, joy and peace but I still imagined it was all about the power. I certainly didn't know the sort of power that the Holy Spirit gives to us.

In the Bible certain gifts are laid out. There are the gifts that God gives to everyone right at the beginning of their life. They are basic gifts, which are spelt out in Romans chapter 12. We have most of these gifts in some small way, but there are those that we're able to act on without even trying. These gifts help us to help each other. There are gifts of insight, serving, teaching, encouraging, contributing, leadership, and mercy.

There is a great story which explains how these gifts complement each other. A group of friends have met up in a hall for a birthday party. As they congregate, the host brings in the cake she has made, but at the threshold she trips and the cake falls into a thousand crumbs. The person who is gifted with insight, known in the Bible as prophesy, says, "I just knew that was going to happen." However, the guy used to serving has dashed off for the dust pan and brush. The teacher stands up and philosophically says, "Now what can we learn from this?" The encourager says, "Well I for one am too full up to eat cake after the great meal you've provided." The person with the gift of contribution has run to the shop for another cake. The leader says with authority, "I will write to the hall committee and tell them they need to do something with that threshold." While the dear one with the gift of compassion is giving the cook a cuddle.

With these gifts, the Holy Spirit encourages us and we soon realise how they work for the common good and strive to use them. The Holy Spirit also shows us how we can be used to build up others and together be a strong community. There is a flip side to these things though as we can misuse them. For instance, an encourager can take someone who serves for granted, or someone with a heart full of mercy can become very cross with those who do not see and act on the need. Those who teach can be scathing of those who don't easily see the facts and the generous can be irate when someone seems stingy. So we need the Holy Spirit, He teaches us to work together, and to strive to obtain at least some of those attributes.

Then there are those gifts that the Holy Spirit gives which are spelt out in 1 Corinthians 12:7-11. They are called spiritual gifts and they're listed like this:- wisdom, knowledge, faith, healing, miraculous powers, prophecy, discernment, speaking in tongues and interpreting tongues. These gifts are like tools, and the Holy Spirit gives them as and when He wishes, they are also for the common good and help us to help others. Through the Holy Spirit we can have the wisdom or knowledge about how to speak or interact with those who we're seeking to help, or just have contact with.

'But the wisdom that comes from heaven is first of all pure; then peace loving, considerate, submissive, full of mercy and good fruit, impartial and sincere. Peacemakers who sow in peace raise a harvest of righteousness.' (James 3:17-18).

To have a special faith which again is a deep knowledge of God's will. To have the faith to pray for healing and to know whether or not things that are said are the truth or a lie. God also uses us, through the power of the Holy Spirit to pray and see Him do amazing things or miracles. The Holy Spirit gives a gift of a heavenly language and also the interpretation of that language.

We need to remember that God is supernatural and so much of our faith is based on the supernatural. I wanted to see all these things happen, miracles of healing and all manner of God's power in my life, to share with others. I have since realised all these things are made possible if we have a relationship with the person of the Holy Spirit as well as Jesus and God the Father. He doesn't want to be used as some sort of magician, but as Holy, ready to love and to be loved. His desire is to help us be like Jesus, and like ourselves, see others touched by His love. He doesn't teach us to do the right thing because of some law, but because the love of God covers everyone, Christian or not, He doesn't have favourites.

Jesus said:- "*If someone needs a coat, give him yours, and your shirt.*" In other words, provide for his needs and make him feel loved.
"*It's easy to love those who love you, but learn to love those who don't, just the same.*"
"*If you have enemies, don't do the same back, pray for them.*"
"*Don't make a public display of praying, just go and have that special time on your own with God.*"
"*You don't get everything you ask for because you ask for the wrong things. Keep asking for the right things, for your Father loves to give you the desires of your heart.*"
"*Don't forget that nothing can separate you from the love of God, however bad it seems, nothing and no one will stop Him loving you.*"
That is the message from the Holy Spirit.

Profile of the Holy Spirit.

A name not often used for the Holy Spirit is Paraclete. Its meaning, as used in the Bible, is the powerful substitute of the physical presence of Jesus. In other words, the Holy Spirit living in each one of us who have asked Him to come, helps us to live as Jesus lived and therefore Jesus lives on, in us. The Holy Spirit brings to us clarity, like suddenly seeing things through a magnifying glass, or hearing and understanding things once hidden. He reminds us of scripture, He convicts us when we do wrong, and He intercedes for us before the Father. He is our advocate, someone who supports us, recommends us and pleads our case. You can't find anything more relational than that can you?

Jesus said, "*I will never leave you or desert you.*" Thank God for that. Even with all of this we are left with questions.

How do you know it is the Holy Spirit and not your own mind telling you what to do?

If you spend time with someone you get to know their voice, very much as a mother knows her own child's cry. Somehow the answers we hear are beyond our own wisdom.

It seems unnatural to be hearing from God.

Yes it does, and it is. God is super-natural and that is always surprising us. The Bible says our ways are not God's ways, so it is different, but God doesn't take us where we aren't ready to go and rarely is God's voice audibly heard – it's more a knowing in your heart.

Wars and horrible things were started because people thought they heard from God.

The Holy Spirit always works in harmony with the Word of God, which is the Scripture. In the same passage that the holiness of the Spirit of God is spelt out, it also speaks of those things that go against the will of God. Among those listed are selfish ambition, fighting and discord. Remember the commandment is to love others as you love yourself, hardly a mandate for war.

Lots of people say things like "God said."

This is why we need the wisdom of the Holy Spirit to know the truth. Many lies are laid at the Lord's door to discredit Him and so we need to be wary. However, the Bible tells us God will give us wisdom when we ask.

PART TWO

TRUTH OF THE MATTER

The family tree.

The first thing that happens when you start to explore Christianity is that you're introduced to the Bible. This is because the Bible is the authority on which Christians base their beliefs. This is all well and good, but as a newcomer to such things, unless you've a good guide, this can be very confusing. Remembering that the theme of this book is our relationship to God and understanding how we fit into the picture. I want to unpack the whole Bible experience a little differently.

There were a lot of Bibles around our family home, sitting in bookcases, usually given as a prize to a family member. They were never read and on the few occasions I did pick one up and flick through it, I would be amazed at the fact it was called the 'Holy' Bible when it was full of wars and disputes. Even though I was educated in a convent school, I was never given, or studied a Bible, only the Catechism. I learnt all about the more popular characters in the Bible, but never understood how their stories were of any consequence to me.

When I was a little girl and went to my Grannies, while she and my mother chatted, they would give me the Victorian cards that my Grandad had sent when his ship called at ports all over the world. I was shocked to see that these cards were very romantic! There was also a huge Bible, it had a table all of its own and in between some pages were leaves of tissue, covering copper print biblical pictures. But best of all, there were pressed flowers and lists of births, marriages and deaths of the members of our family, members that I knew little or nothing about. They, like my grandmother, had obviously had a history and part of that history was mine too.

The Bible is a bit like that. Most times before we have started on our voyage of discovery, the Bible is something we've only had snatches of, stories that have been told to us that don't hold together in some real way. The book sits on the bookshelf and often is only looked at in passing (if at all), with all those important people staying locked within its pages, along with the very personal family history.

Of course the scriptures aren't easy to understand, how could they be? The Bible is actually sixty six books written by different authors. The first thirty nine Old Testament books cover the story of creation, the flood and the subsequent two thousand years. They cover personal and national history, but also prophecy, poetry and wisdom.

The geography of the story in the Old Testament is set in the Middle East and takes in countries as we know them now, Egypt, Lebanon, Israel, Jordan, Palestine, Cyprus, Syria, Assyria, Iraq, and Iran. It is little wonder we find it hard to keep up with! At the end of those two thousand years there is a four hundred year gap, during which time nothing is recorded about anything God is saying.

Then we have the New Testament. The four Gospels, followed by the Acts of the Apostles after the death and resurrection of Jesus. Then there's Epistles (or letters) sent by the Apostles. It finishes with the prophetic book Revelation. These writings cover the journeys made by the Apostles to all the nearby regions and covers areas all around the Mediterranean Sea as far away as Rome.

A message from the past.

So where do we fit into all of this history? Isn't the Bible an account of the people of Israel? Yes, it is, but the whole Bible, Old Testament and New, holds a message for us personally. We've a personal connection to the main theme that runs throughout. A theme of love and redemption, that runs through the history of time, but is often hidden by the circumstances of that period. Have you ever watched that TV programme - 'Who do you think you are?' where famous people research their family tree? It's wonderful for the participant to find out when a particular ancestor had made a significant mark in their lives, but also surprisingly often to find that there is someone who has had a somewhat seedier or impoverished background. It's even more exciting when the records search back into the distant past to find intrigue and possibly even uncover traditions that we could never imagine in our lives. So why wouldn't we find all sorts of difficult stuff in the Bible? Stuff that God never intended and called on His children to change, but nevertheless it makes the story difficult for us to digest. However, when God's children were willing to change their minds', He was too and He rescued them from the plight they found themselves in, changing the course of history.

The Jews were a people whose patriarch, Abraham, had a relationship with God. Abraham listened, believed and obeyed God. God called him a friend and even changed his name from Abram to

Abraham, meaning 'father of many.' God desired that he and his family would be a special people, living in relationship with Him and enjoying His love and favour. Abraham's grandson Jacob would also have a miraculous encounter with God and subsequently had his name changed to Israel. The Bible then documents the journey of Israel, the now nation, throughout the following ages. After Jacob returns from Paddam Aram, God appeared to him again and blessed him. God said to him;-

"'Your name is Jacob, but you will no longer be called Jacob; your name will be Israel." So He named him Israel. And God said to him, "I am God Almighty; be fruitful and increase in number. A nation and a community of nations will come from you, and kings will come from your body.'" (Genesis 35:10-11).

This is the beginning of the story of a chosen people and incorporates all those Bible stories we are taught, as well as many other details. However, the thread running throughout is still of a Father God whose desire is to see His children returned to Him to live in a righteous manner. A God and Father who went to great lengths to reach His people, using prophets to set out the consequences of their actions should they not turn around from living in an ungodly way. It's not always a pleasant read and as throughout we see God's enemy fights to change the nature of His people, to bring down and destroy the relationship of a Father and His family. Certainly the characters were far from your image of saintly people. Even the heroes might be worthy of having criminal records, but that is exactly why God is so necessary and why the Bible says so much about us. God in the continuing story of the Bible, reprimands, punishes, forgives and redeems – but, always, always loves.

For some years Roger and I ran a house which gave supported housing to mainly young men who were suffering with addictions. It was interesting, but terribly sad in so many cases, to observe the journey they had in their close relationships. Some parents could not bear to see their children going to extreme lengths, even stealing to maintain their drug use. They'd forgive them when they stole from them, manipulating them for their own ends and were, in some cases, willing to supply them with money so they wouldn't break the law. Eventually though the dear souls would have to give up and leave their beloved children to their fate. It was the only way, even though it broke their hearts to do it.

The awful truth is that addiction turns people into someone that they don't want to be and a child that the parents often don't recognise. This didn't mean the parents gave up on them. In fact they'd frequently contact us, trying to find other ways their children could make their way back to normality. It's a bit like the story in the Bible which tells of children who've become people God never intended them to be. But even though their relationship with God became broken, He never stopped loving them or crying for them to come back to His arms. Unfortunately, there came a time when He had to stop His intervention, by doing so allowed their enemies (just as drugs are an enemy) to overpower them, taking the risk that they might not recover.

Lastly, I need to mention an all important part of the jigsaw, the correlation of the relationship and journey of Israel to God, just like our own personal relationship and journey. Those battles of things like greed, lust, sadness or rejection that can consume our lives, aren't so easily defined and often, just like the Israelites are made through our own fault. The response of our Father is the same today as it was then. The truth of it still sets us free if we obey it. Jesus and the Holy Spirit, came to enable us not to make the same mistakes of the ill-fated Jews, but to understand more clearly the traps and pitfalls that lead to sin and destruction.

We lived in Australia during the years my children were growing up. The schools had a practice of having a period each week called 'Show and Tell.' The children took in various items they thought had particular importance to show the class and tell their class mates about. This sometimes became much more than showing pictures of their pet or talking about what sort of day out they had with Mum and Dad. I would cringe sometimes at the things my kids revealed about our family life and thought the teachers had a really good time in discovering all the skeletons that were let out of the cupboard by the innocent children, much to the parent's discomfort. My children recounting the highlights of their upbringing couldn't have shown an accurate picture of all the intricacies that made up the life we actually led. However, the Bible does track the most important messages and theme that runs throughout the whole book is the constant love and faithfulness of God to the people that He has chosen to be His representatives and family. Jesus is the authority of the whole Bible and we should start with His take on the life that God the

Father had intended for us all. We'll find if we do, just like my Grannie, He throws light on all the hidden meaning of being part of this amazing dynasty.

Have you ever tried to find Wally? You know the boy in a red and white hooped jumper hidden in a picture filled with people and events. As we scrutinise the picture, eventually we'll find Wally in there somewhere. By searching the scriptures in the same way, we'll find Jesus. It's as though the most highly acclaimed people in the Bible are imitating in some way the character of Jesus. How could they imitate Him, if He hadn't been born? It is as though the footprint of Christ is in each and every generation, an expression of hope, a promise of their future redemption. The Psalmist sings of Jesus, Solomon writes love letters portraying Him and Elijah and Elisha perform the miracles He will also do. Why then did He delay so long in coming? Isaiah was the prophet who most clearly proclaimed the coming of the Messiah, His life and death.

'Surely he took up our infirmities and carried our sorrows, yet we considered Him stricken by God, smitten by Him and afflicted. But He was pierced for our transgressions, He was crushed for our iniquities; the punishment that

brought us peace was upon Him, and by His wounds we are healed. We are like sheep who have gone astray, each have turned to his own way; and the Lord has laid on Him the iniquity of us all.' (Isaiah 53:4-6).

Timing.

It's my belief, that our understanding of timing makes it very difficult for us to properly understand the works of the Lord God Almighty. If you're going to believe in Him, you have to concede the fact that He has a handle on it all. Our time and His time are just not the same. It's as though all of this passage of time told in the Bible is happening at the same time! God is seeing the beginning and the end all at once and so even though we've the right to write our own story, God has already read it before it is written! There are many examples of this, when God seems to use even the worst time for the best outcome, turning men who are going the wrong way into giants of faith and victory. People taken captive, people of dubious parentage, all sorts of people change because of God's gracious intervention.

I love the story of Job. Poor old Job, once favoured, was suddenly picked on by Satan. Satan says to

God:- "*Your boy that you love so much is only like that because You are looking after him all the time. Take away Your protection and he will soon turn to my way of thinking.*" (Job 1:8-12, my paraphrase).

So God agrees, sure in the strength and commitment of His dear son and servant Job. During this whole book, Job is bombarded with ill health and suffering, not to mention those so called friends, who take much pleasure telling him how they would have handled the whole thing better. Job is naturally rather harassed so takes God to task! But here is the Father's voice.

"*Where were you when I laid the earths foundation? Tell me, if you understand, who marked off its dimensions? Surely you know!*" (Job 38:4-5).

In other words, 'I know better than you.' God restored to Job all he had lost, and I'm sure that Job learnt and was blessed by understanding God and life in a deeper way through the trials that he suffered. So God has the right to change the script. The story of Job would have strengthened and encouraged thousands of people who believe that they'd been abandoned by God. Nothing is ever wasted and the Bible is the confirmation of the perfect plan of a perfect Father.

Trust.

The heat went on, no sign of rain and every blade was dry.
The sun like a red hot orb hung low and burning in the sky.
The desert floor was cracked and broken, a stony wilderness,
even thorny bushes need water to exist.

Now if you are lost in a wilderness during the dry season and
you come across a fruit filled tree, you'll want to know the reason.
You'll want to find the water that makes the tree so green.
You'll want to know what makes this tree the best you have ever seen.

But if you are in a forest where the trees are tall and strong,
you'll never stop to wonder where they get their water from.

So if you ever get a chance of being planted like a tree,
you had better choose a desert so everyone can see.

For there will be no need to worry when it's hot or when its dry,
for your roots will go down to the water and your branches will reach to the sky.
For when you are planted by the Lord, no matter where you be,
You'll be watered by a river of love, and you will grow, just like a tree!   Jill Boyton

I include this poem as an adaptation of Jeremiah 17:7-8 which to me encourages us to believe that God can use all things, time or circumstances for good.

Hidden treasure.

I hate computers. I wish you could be here now to hear me complaining about the one I am using to write this. However, you'd have to be a fool not to be aware of the immense opportunities of using the internet. The Bible is like a computer. You can treat it in several different ways. You can refuse to open its pages and embrace its content and opportunity.

You can use it, as a handy tool, flicking to the bits you understand but not knowing really how it works. Or you can completely familiarise yourself with all applications and capability, learn from others and experience the benefits it brings. The Bible is so much like this. There are those that try to quote chapter and verse with only the information they've picked up from a random selection of Bible references. There are those who stick to the way they know the Bible, not exploring the further implications of the meaning. Then there are those who dare to spend time unravelling the message and find a whole raft of stuff that was hidden in that ordinary looking book.

I remember the excitement of receiving a letter back from my pen pal after I had written to her. There's something special about a letter compared to using Facebook, Twitter or email. Yes, it's more laborious and it takes commitment to keep up, but I always found letters the most exciting way to build up a relationship with your pal. It was easier to tell all, when the person you were writing to wasn't in a position to be gossiping to your family, etc. You also learnt about their culture, which seemed less foreign when your friend was writing about all the things they did. The Bible, if you spend time thinking about it, becomes your friend. The voice of Jesus speaks through the pages to you in a personal way. This book of the history of ancient beginnings becomes relevant and real to you today.

The Bible is indeed a unique book, a book with many faces. Like the wardrobe in the Lion, the Witch and the Wardrobe, you have to climb into the ordinary cupboard, pull back the garments of this world and open the door to step into the very different but very real world of Narnia.

The Bible says faith comes from hearing the Word of God. So just as the more you read your letters from your pen pal you hear their voice, and come to know them, so the more you read the Bible you understand and come to know God in a way you wouldn't have thought possible. When reading the Bible we mustn't forget that first and foremost it is a spiritual book. Many of its writings are like three sided mirror, one affirming the past, another shining a light on the future, and the other looking straight into the present. A book of hidden treasure that even the likes of you and me can find if we really try.

Even with all of this we are left with questions.

Science now gives us information on the ages that it took for the world as we know it to be formed, so how are we expected to believe what the Bible tells us?

This is a tough one, but the Bible tells us that the world was 'created' not 'formed,' and tells us specifically what 'form' this creation took. We know that it took God six days, and it would appear that the order in which this is recorded isn't so removed from how the scientist would understand the physics. Our difficulty is that we've a limited conception of time and dimension. Whilst scientists continue to push the boundaries of our understanding on the vastness of the universe, with the immense knowledge about particles and matter, there are many Christian scientists who would argue the facts and have published findings of their own. Even with all these facts we're on the brink of destroying the very planet we want to discover the origin of. It begs the question, if we earnestly pursued the dynamic of holy spirituality in Christ, rather than answer the question of how we came to exist, wouldn't we be thinking about how we can continue to live, in the manner God desires us to, in peace and love!

What about prehistoric man, evolution and how it measures up to the creation story?

It would be facile to come up with all sorts of answers to this question in the face of so much emerging evidence. However, what baffles me is the difference in time, place, and physical type the prehistoric finds take. The temptation is to liken these 'men' to animals in the process of evolution, but their environment and occupation seems to make it more complicated than that. Also why are apes still on earth if by the progression of evolution they took on human form? I'm no expert and concede that a good deal of faith has to be applied to the subject, but I prefer to believe that mankind as we know it, was God breathed. In other words, God breathed life into Adam and he became the forbearer of the human race, able to make moral choices and to recognise his relationship with God. He was given the place of appreciating nature whilst knowing not just 'mother nature' but 'Father God' the Creator. History tells us that the beginnings of the ancient civilisations began in the fertile crescent, an area of land encompassing Mesopotamia, and Egypt, reaching from the river Nile, to the plains surrounding the Tigris and Euphrates. It's here the Garden of Eden would have been placed, and Israel is squashed into the middle of it. Do I believe that Adam and Eve were created there? The answer for me is 'yes.'

What makes the Bible different from any other 'holy' book?

The Bible calls itself the Truth. Man has always been caught up in a tissue of lies. We have pursued the world of legends, superstition, myths and mysticism. We enjoy dabbling in the unknown. However, the Bible is clear. It's the unfolding of the dynamic of true love and love's source, the power of God. He doesn't have to hide in mystery and tells us, He is the light. There is no darkness, no hidden corners of delusion. He also assures us that if we search for the real truth we'll find it in Him. That is of course whether or not we want to 'look'.

The unique and central message of the Bible is the message of salvation through grace. Not through law, not by man's contriving or striving, but only God's grace through the death and resurrection of Christ. It's the easiest message to understand, but perhaps the hardest to come to terms with. The fact that God desires to forgive us on the basis that we believe in the redeeming work of Jesus on the cross, and not our own ability to make our way into everlasting life.

With so many authors how can we believe it isn't somehow selected to hang together?

Do you know this is one of the things that makes my faith stronger. It would be impossible for a book written by so many, over such a long period of time, to come together in such a precise way. To have so many voices, stories and prophecies and yet stick to the central theme throughout. It never ceases to amaze me that one piece of scripture can say so many things to the reader and for it all to be relevant to the text. It's not just a book that you study, it's a book for life. It's not one that you live for, it's one that you live by. It's the Word of God, so it is not just a book, it's a person. Read it and tell me what you think!

Reference: Genesis Chapter 1&2, Matthew 7:24-29.

IS IT FAIR?

Justice.

As I walked down the streets of this small French village I cried. The thought of the carnage this peaceful place witnessed on the 10th June 1944 was unbearable. As retribution to a deed carried out by the French Resistance, or an act of defiance by an angry member of the public, the commander of an SS German Army Unit (Wiermachte) rounded up all 642 men, women and children of Oradour-sur-Glane and killed them in cold blood. The sadness and injustice of it all overwhelmed me.

To add to the pain of that horrendous act, amazingly the war crimes of these terrible murderers went unpunished. The burnt out remains of the village are left untouched for the thousands of visitors to receive a reminder of the way in which man can be so evil and vicious to his own kind. When faced with such atrocities, once again we cry:- "Where was God?", "Where was justice?"

When Roger and I became the managers of the house intended for homeless and needy people, we'd never had any dealings with those suffering with addictions and were naively unaware of the need for housing among people with these difficulties. Unfortunately, our understanding was based on our belief that most addicts follow a life of crime, which affects us all in one way or another, so when judgement is passed they should take the penalties our society deems right and proper. Yet, those years of living and working with those who needed support, mainly through the result of drugs, became the most informative and precious period of my life. Never had I felt such love for those who were really strangers to me. Never, after all sorts of encounters in my Christian experience, had I felt the closeness of God so much. I came to understand the hearts of those I supported. Some definitely needed to have some kind of punishment for their bad behaviour. Others were more the victims than the perpetrators of crime. Who could be the judge? I'm certainly glad I wasn't.

I understood for the first time that when God tells us the only people that we should judge are ourselves, He was right. Those soldiers who used Ordour-sur-Glane as a killing field had themselves come back from the Russian front where unimaginable horrors were perpetrated. The minds and spirits of those involved would have been more than gravely marked by their experiences. Each war or conflict is made up of individuals who have their own story, maybe their own conflicts.

'Do not judge or you too will be judged. For in the same way you judge others you will be judged; and with the measure you use, it will be measured to you.' (Matthew 7:1-2).

All through history, mankind has been caught up in this perpetual power game. From despots who control and destroy their own kind, to so called democratic governments who are so involved with financial considerations or party politics, that they lose sight of their main objective the well-being of others.

If God is God why does He allow unjust situations like wars and illness to rule over us? Well exactly, the answer is in that question, who does rule over us? Is it God? You may be surprised to know that the scriptures say that Satan is the ruler of this world. He brought the temptation of rebellion and disobedience to Adam and Eve, so that when the first of mankind chose to accept it, he won the right to rule them. With our own freewill we gave him the mandate to take over. If we look, we can see the consequences of that choice all around us and throughout history. However, most of the time we surround ourselves with distractions that make us feel that all is right with the world. A new car, perhaps a holiday, or a new TV - anything that gives us the 'feel good factor' and keeps us from dwelling on the truth, that all is certainly not 'right with the world.'

The truth of the matter is that all of mankind is caught up with 'things', often outside our control, but have the power to govern the path of our lives and the lives of those around us. Those 'things' include, greed, power, anger, etc. Attributes in direct contradiction to those of the Holy Spirit we mentioned in the earlier chapter. Without others who share the same understanding and will to stand against injustice, recognising the ills that blight our lives lie within each soul, we too can be sucked into a place of indifference or confusion.

Who are we?

I spent a lot of time working in the care profession and there is something refreshing about being around people with profound needs. You see no-one knows anything about you in those surroundings. Everyone has the same uniform - a uniform of need, compassion and hope. No-one knows or cares about how rich you are, what qualifications you have or your social standing. In these circumstances, the real thing that life is about is underlined. Through love, relationship, understanding and companionship, both those in need and those who offer help, are transformed in the time they are together, into a community that understands and responds with respect, without having to think about it.

Here is the best comparison we have to the place of Jesus within our world. He appears in the A&E department of life, not to care about all the outward trappings of who we are, but the real us, the us in pyjamas with all the frills thrown aside. He wants us to be real, not to treat us as some accident or charity case but to have relationship with us and to deal with our hurts and pain from the injustice we've suffered or recognise. Each of us will need different treatment, some healing, some forgiveness, some to be equipped to help others. But to each of us, Jesus brings the answer we're looking for in life and with and through Him compassion overcomes injustice.
This is difficult to accept, but Jesus said, we're in this world but not of it. We grapple with the inconsistencies of life.

Here, today, the sun is shining, spring is coming and it's a lovely day. However, right now, a whole nation is battling with its survival, after a huge earthquake and tsunami, and radiation leakage, and it's snowing!!! Christians don't lead charmed lives they can suffer the same consequences as others. After all, God loves us all! But if that is so, why do the innocent suffer? Why do some have blessings in life while others starve to death? God must be to blame, right? It always pains me to hear those who place those inconceivable unjust things in life at the feet of God. Partly because the Bible teaches that the creation that God made suffers and groans under the same tyrannical regime as we do. God's best intentions for man have been corrupted.

'I consider that our present sufferings are not worth comparing with the glory that will be revealed in us. The creation waits in eager expectation for the sons of God to be revealed. For the creation was subjected to frustration, not by its own choice, but by the will of the one who subjected it, in hope that the creation itself will be liberated from its bondage to decay, and brought into the glorious freedom of the children of God.' (Romans 8:18-20).

Secondly, Jesus came for just this reason, displaying by His life and death, that injustice and suffering were His as well as ours. Also, that He overcame those things by His own righteousness and forgiveness. There are those we know of, who have held the place of respect and honour in society. Martin Luther King Jr., Ghandi, Nelson Mandela, all who have chosen to suffer instead of retaliate. Their peaceful protest, though costly, proved to turn the society in which they lived, around to reconciliation. They believed that the goodness of each soul could overcome and make a difference to the whole of mankind. If we look through history, it's not those who've walked in the way of wickedness that we remember and revere – it's those who have single handedly turned the tide of wickedness and injustice.

Christians do believe in life after death though, despite the evil and suffering in this world, death has lost its sting. It's the doorway to life, life in all its fullness. As I write this, it all seems terribly naive and unrealistic in the face of so much pain. I have, as most of my fellow Christians, seen and suffered pain, loss and injustice. But what I can tell you is that Jesus walks through these times with us, making it easier to bear. He often turns individual suffering into something deeper and more significant in the victim's life; an inspiration and hope to those who look on.

It's in this world that we choose what our life will be in the next. If we choose to follow the ways of sin then we're asking for that environment to be the place to which we go. If we choose the way of love, peace and righteousness then, through Jesus, that will be our hope and future. But we can be assured that those who perpetrate evil get the fair judgement they deserve and the cries of those who have suffered have been heard.

Of course there has to be justice now and a system with laws to bring people to account. However, justice walks a narrow path through retaliation, revenge and vendettas, which is why it's better to wait on God to be the judge. We still encounter and suffer the same evil ways that have been perpetrated throughout history. We watch the suffering, the terrible fate of innocents who suffer, the same inhumane and unjust fate as the people of Oradour-sur-Glane. But we need to ask ourselves, 'do we have a part to play in the unfairness of it all?' Thankfully, there are those who, through self-sacrifice and their own personal suffering, are prepared to either fight for justice or walk hand in hand with those most afflicted in this world. Many of these are not believers and it would be wrong to not applaud the amazing work they're doing. Although, I am sure Jesus longs for them to hear Him say, *'Well done good and faithful servant.' (Matthew 25:21)*.

I'm aware that religion has been among the worst perpetrators of deeds of evil throughout time. This has been the reason for good men to turn away from the Church, disbelieving in a just God. Religion and politics have always formed the basis of man's most passionate opinions, neither of which have anything to do with the will of God. As I hope we covered in the first chapter, Christianity should be all about a loving relationship with God, not a religious practice of man's interpretation of holy laws. God isn't impressed with religion, only with our desire to follow and worship Him and live loving other as we love ourselves. It must be a great source of pain for Him to see how man has allowed evil to pervert all Jesus came to bring through His life, death and resurrection. Therefore, ultimately Christians believe that justice belongs to the Lord and retribution will be given to those who suffer at the hands of evil men.

Repentance.

Repentance is one of those old fashioned words that's barely used outside of Christian circles any more. Remorse or regret are the words we tend to use instead. However, repentance means more than this. The actual meaning is to 'turn away.' Within the context of scripture it doesn't mean to apologise, but more mourn, or grieve over that which is wrong. Either for those things which we've done ourselves or those which have been done by others. I always think that humility has to play a big part in repentance. The Bible tells us if we humble ourselves and admit our wrong to God, He will hear and forgive us (1 John 1:8-9).

The other factor, of course, is to own up to anything we've done wrong and anyone we've offended and be ready to pay the consequences. I've done too many things wrong to account for them here and it wouldn't make good reading, but to illustrate what I mean I will recount an embarrassing time when I was well and truly caught out.

Over the years we owned several VW Camper vans which we used to take our family away in. We enjoyed the freedom it brought us, however, this also meant that we had to use them as our family car which I often had to drive. One morning I was running late taking my youngest boy to school. As I drove through the cars parked on each side of the road I felt quite flustered at not being able to find a suitable place to park. In my haste I heard a knock, but as I looked through the mirror could see nothing so drove on. As I stopped and organised my son a young man came running up and said, "You've just knocked the mirror off my van!" Without a pause to think, I said emphatically that I hadn't. He retaliated that he had witnesses to say that I did. I flounced off with my lad, not giving the chap a second glance. Now away from the scene of the crime I cringed with embarrassment and regret. How could I so blatantly deny something I knew I had done? I was a Christian! This wasn't the behaviour my father expected of me and I was aware that I had not only embarrassed myself but God as well. I went back to where the man was waiting for me. "I'm so sorry," I said, "I'm a Christian and I know that denying what I did was really wrong and of course I'll pay for the damage." I'm sure he felt like saying "Whoa, OK lady, no need to go over the top." As it was, I never heard from him again.

The Bible says that we encounter angels unawares, I wonder if he was one sent to show me what I was capable of. The point is though that my sin wasn't to do with the mirror but the fact that I'd committed an act of deceit and injustice by lying. In other words, I'd jumped camp and was fraternising with the enemy! It sounds over the top but I had lied, caused the guy an injustice and I was disobedient. Jesus said to "love others as yourself" and I didn't. He was just as much a child of God as me and it grieves our Father when one child is rotten to the other.

God speaks to the nation of Israel in the Old Testament and tells them to repent. While, in the New Testament the call to repentance is addressed as more personal. In each case the response causes a deep remorse, in fact mourning is more appropriate as it signifies a loss. When we do things that are wrong, we lose our integrity, our peace, our moral compass. But most importantly if we lose our connection with God, it leaves us spiritually dead. Each time we do wrong and don't repent, it makes repeating the act easier and somehow blinds us to our wrongdoing. That is why the scriptures record God calling, calling, calling; "Come back to Me." Repentance, turning from wrong and always intending to do so, gives us the way back and restores our connection with God.

The cost.

Years ago when my daughter was a teenager we had a 'Mum versus teenager' confrontation. She and her friend had been on a shopping spree in preparation for a night out at the end of term, then on to her friends for the night, which I felt uneasy about. The dress that she had bought to wear was extremely inappropriate and there was no way I was going to allow her to go out in it without severe disagreement. I explained to her that my objection was because I didn't want her to appear anything other than she was, a lovely young beautiful girl, with no need to add something so dramatic to the mix. Sadly her friend was party to the ensuing argument, but I stood my ground while doors slammed and shouting ensued. After a while, as I folded my ironing and put it away, I heard her say to her friend, "I know she's right, she's only saying it because she loves me." What joy I felt. Not because I had won the day but because she knew my heart and that I cared for her well-being.

Father God is so much more loving and only wants what's right for us. Even though there was certainly no sin, we need to be careful we aren't influenced by opinion of others, which can lead us into a dangerous place. Unfortunately, there was a cost, the dress, half the dance missed and humiliation in front of her friend, all of which I regretted terribly. But there often is a cost to standing up for what's right. That's why I believe parents often do their children a favour by being strong about their behaviour. It gives our children a way out. They can't do whatever they like, as Mum or Dad wouldn't be happy. The responsibility is taken by the parent and the child is set free of the blame of not conforming. We need to have boundaries. We need to have a Father that says "No." Not because of any other thing apart from His loving protection. Those things that may not be considered wrong or bad of themselves but hold a risk of developing into something outside our control, we can be protected from. Will we listen and change tack? Turn away from those things we do wrong and listen to our Dad, Father God? I would like to think the issue of the dress brought my daughter and me closer. And if I didn't buy her a new dress, I should have done. God loves to reward an obedient child.

Forgiveness.

Forgiveness is something, as you can imagine, God is quite hot on. We all know how it works. If you're the one who needs forgiveness you think it's a good thing. If you're the one who has suffered the consequences you aren't so quick to reciprocate. I guess it says it all in the Lord's Prayer doesn't it? *'Forgive us our sins as we forgive those who sin against us.'* At this point I gulp. All those times I hold grudges towards those who have in some way offended me. Jesus said a servant isn't above his master. In other words, if He can forgive in such magnitude don't you think that we should do the same?

Jesus on the cross cried out to His Father, "Father, forgive them, they no not what they do." In that moment Jesus released pardon for all our sin and crime as He took the punishment for it on His shoulders on the cross. The only requirement made to us, is that we received it and in doing so received Him also, as our redeemer.

Some years ago I was unfairly misrepresented and betrayed by people that I loved and believed loved me. The distress and pain I felt made me quite ill.

After some time had passed and I had licked my wounds, reconciliation took place and I thought I had forgiven those involved. However, every time a name was mentioned or a detail connected to that time was raised, I was filled with resentment, rage even. I prayed and prayed telling God I had forgiven them, but still I was plagued with unforgiveness. Then one day I felt that God showed me that I too had committed the same sort of sin. Maybe unnoticed, maybe not in the same way, but the same intention and with the same heart. I knew I had to repent and as I did the whole thing lifted away and never returned. The point is that all the time there's a foothold for sin to destroy us in some way, it will.

So do we have to tolerate abuse and forgive? Of course not. But removing yourself from the situation, or by seeking help doesn't mean that you don't forgive. Jesus said it's easy to love those who are good to you, but He tells us to love our enemies also. That starts with forgiveness.

Corrie ten Boom was a Dutch Christian who lived in Amsterdam during the Nazi occupation. Along with her father and sister they sheltered and aided many Jews who were being hounded out and arrested. Eventually they too were captured and taken to concentration camps. Corrie never saw her father again. She and her sister stayed together but her sister was much weaker than she was and didn't recover from the harsh treatment they had to endure. During one working expedition her sister was beaten so badly that she subsequently died, beforehand though she begged Corrie not to hold any hatred against their attackers. Corrie survived by amazing miracles and went on to preach forgiveness and reconciliation.

At one such rally, a Nazi officer known to be from those most cruel, came to the front and told her he had become a Christian and told her how sorry he was for the things he had done. Corrie said that her hand felt like lead and she had difficulty shaking the hand that had perpetrated such cruelty. However, that action had brought Jesus to the man that day, reaching out in love to cover his wrongdoing. The evil had been broken, the repentance and forgiveness had restored love and peace. This is the message of the cross and the answer to injustice.

Freedom.

Forgiveness is a powerful tool to freedom. Imagine you have two index files that represent you, and that every piece of information that's fed to you is placed in one of those files - the information that's forgiving and the information that isn't. These files are your memory, they record every word and act that's said and done to you and they're the basis on which you draw the impression of yourself and those you interact with. Every unkind word is recorded, every deed is set down. Each time you close the file you can't see it. But as soon as one more entry is made your anger is kindled and the sticking plaster which you put over the wound is ripped off.

Often the file with the negative information is much fuller than the positive, which can make you feel very unhappy. You may start hitting back, matching the emotion which you received. You may feel diminished and depressed. These things you've stored have a profound effect on the way you function and think about life, even when you've hidden them in the 'file'.

So what's the key? How can you concentrate on the positive file and not let the negative spoil the peace and love that should be yours? You de-clutter.

We've all had a clean out – for example the loft or cupboard under the stairs. And we've all known how liberating it is when you've finished the task.
It's the same with your files. Hard though it is, you pull out each file, forgive the person who has sinned against you and tear up the incriminating information. Steadily you clear out each negative and harmful thought as it is revealed to you, until there are no more names or words left, then watch as your positive file grows.

When the time comes for us to meet with Jesus, He'll open your files and He will judge each person whose name is held within them. Where necessary, He'll give retribution to those who have need of it. Let's hope we've torn up every file in our unforgiveness box and not held anything against anyone. In fact let's bless them and allow them to be reconciled to God. Now we're free – free to be all that God wants us to be. But a word of warning, will your name or mine be in anyone else's negative file? Perhaps we'd better say sorry to them!

'Again Jesus said to them, "Peace be with you! As the Father has sent me, I am sending you." And with that He breathed on them and said "Receive the Holy Spirit. If you forgive anyone his sins, they are forgiven; if you do not forgive them, they are not forgiven."' (John 20:21-23).

Often it's ourselves that we find it hard to forgive for the things we've done. We believe we shouldn't be liked and should be punished, so we harbour brokenness of heart. How well God understands this, He doesn't want us to be held by memories of our misdoing but only to remember the truth of His amazing grace. So He tears up our record when we repent and throws it away, as far as the East is from the West. He doesn't condemn, His dearest wish is that we live full and happy lives, so we can forgive others, and forgive ourselves.

'He does not treat us as our sins deserve or repay us according to our iniquities. For as high as the heavens are above the earth, so great is His love for those who fear Him, as far as the east is from the west, so far has He removed our transgressions from us.' (Psalm 103:10-12).

Even with all of this we are left with questions.

You say that God has to allow man free will. But not everything that brings suffering is due to bad men. What about natural disasters?

If you don't believe in the story of Adam and Eve, the temptation and ultimate victory of Satan over man, it's difficult to equate the two. In John 12:13, Jesus says that Satan is the ruler of this world and that brings judgement to the earth. In Ephesians 6:12 Paul says that the struggles aren't with men, but with the spiritual forces of darkness which we're subject to. In other words, there's a spiritual war that rages. It causes not only wars and disputes of all kinds, but also the nature of the world created by God, to be perverted by sin. I didn't believe all this stuff when I first became a Christian. I found this all too much to contemplate. I think this is O.K. We can only trust in our faith in Christ and He's the one who reveals the truth to us. However, as we've already discussed, it doesn't take much for any person, (Christian or not) to see the severe pressure the climate and ecology of the world is under, and the practices of evil, etc. Therefore, it causes us to wonder whether these things are caused by man's inability to live in a way that preserves the ordained laws of a righteous God, who wants us to have the values for which we were designed.

Why are all the so called bad things nice?

That's a question I might ask every time I eat a cream bun and know it's going to my waist line and give me heartburn. Not fair is it?! Things that give me pleasure actually do me harm as well. Contrary to common belief, God isn't a spoil-sport. But we can tell the things that aren't good by the way they trap us. They're going to be 'nice' otherwise they wouldn't tempt us. For example, Sexual sin cannot only lead to disease, breakdown of relationships and abuse, but all sorts of other related problems. Habits that pander to our desires in excessive and dangerous ways can trap us into a life of unhappiness. All those things we do wrong come at a price. Often one we can't afford. However, we can find extreme happiness and fulfilment through wholesome and beautiful things. For instance I might find watching marathons inspiring. There are all sorts of people running for fun, but who've also disciplined their bodies to be able to do something of great value to themselves and others.

How can not having forgiveness for someone who has harmed you in some awful way, be wrong?

Jesus taught that if God can forgive the debt we owe, by making recompense possible through the death of His son, we too can forgive even the most dreadful sin. But this isn't all that forgiveness means. Unforgiveness allows bitterness, anger, brokenness and revenge to destroy the peace of our minds, hearts and bodies. I don't believe for one moment that forgiveness is a moment of goodwill that sets everything back to normal. Or that the injured party doesn't mourn and weep for the injustice they feel. God loves us though and He doesn't want the original wrong to do even more damage to us through our hard line approach. Ultimately it's Jesus who helps us to forgive as He has forgiven us. A sentiment we've often spoken when praying the Lord's Prayer.

A QUESTION OF BELIEF

Complete trust or confidence in someone or something.

Have you ever really pondered about what 'faith' is? Not just as a religious belief but as part of our understanding. I certainly had never thought of it in terms of relationship until I read 1 Corinthians 13:12-13. It says something profound about faith. Paul starts off by saying that we can't see spiritual things clearly, a bit like peering through a mist. However, before long the sun will shine and we will see and know God as clearly as He sees and knows us. But for now there are the three things we do to lead us on to completeness. Trust steadily in God, hope unswervingly and love extravagantly. Could this statement spell out an integral part of our make up as human beings I wonder? If you look at the three responses Paul mentions, the greatest undoubtedly is love. We can appreciate that if not love as we experience it, animals have a strong connection with their own kind and even with us. It's as though there is an undefined, underpinning of love throughout all of life. Faith and hope don't connect themselves with emotion as love does, yet they're mentioned along with love as the three remaining elements of our spirituality. So how does faith link up with love?

Faith and hope are more a result of decision. After all, we have to exercise faith with all sorts of things – for example when we first set foot on a plane. We base our hope on the data we have, we believe the aircraft and its pilot are capable of transporting us safely to our destination, so we put our faith in the information we have. Why would we do that? I guess the answer is because our desire to get to our destination is great. We know nothing about aviation or the pilot but we exercise our faith and go. It seems as though faith is informed gambling, linked with a desire for the end result. If it wasn't for faith we wouldn't carry out a million and one tasks – from taking our first step, to spending years studying for a degree. Faith is a fact of life. What makes the difference is where we put our faith and for what reason.

'Now faith is being sure of what we hope for and certain of what we do not see.' (Hebrews 11:1).

The most important use of faith is in those we're closest to. We believe in them and trust that they would never betray us. Yet what grief we cause each other when we don't live up to the expectations and commitment portrayed. The damage this causes when those who we've loved and trusted have in some way damaged us. Will we ever be able to trust anyone again? Can it be worth loving someone and believing they'll always love us? So there is a great link between love and faith!

Fear is the block to stepping out into the realms of faith. Fear that you're wasting your time. Fear that this is all going to go wrong and something terrible will happen. The Bible teaches us that *'Perfect love casts out fear.'* Here the scripture makes the connection with love. We know that God is perfect love, our trust and faith in Him is not misplaced.

Why am I discussing this with you? Because the first step to finding out anything about Christianity takes a certain amount of faith, even risk. Most of the things which are entailed in learning about Christianity aren't seen. No-one could blame us if we refused to take on board those beliefs, which could prove to be a lot of highly charged nonsense without explanation. Christians aren't good at putting out information that you need to know to reassure you. We so often forget that the language we use can leave others feeling even more confused.

So what are the safety checks for faith you'd employ? Most likely information and experience. If the airline you're thinking of flying with has a good safety record and your friends have recommended them, you'll feel more inclined to trust your flight to them. Likewise in your relationships, your faith to rely on your parent, partner or friend will grow as your love and experience assures you of their steadfast character. In the same way, our ability to step out into the realms of faith regarding Christianity are influence by our experience of love and the facts we're supplied with.

Maybe it would be the love of God your friends display or their stories of how God has loved them. Would that be your point of reference? Or a look at the Bible, if you're brave enough, some research at the local church or a Christian group? Whichever you choose, this would be a start at building our faith and filling in the blank spaces. Prepare to be surprised at the amazing things God does when we believe in Him, even when we're weak.

When our children were small they had a pre-bed ritual. They would go to bed and have a story, then when they were all supposed to be tucked up, they'd get up and run in together. Feigning surprise my husband would gather them up, one on his shoulders and the others hanging on and he would run at the door only ducking at the last minute. I would hold my breath, they had to do it one more time before they would settle, fighting for the most risky position. I don't think I need to explain the comparison!

Love and grace.

It's interesting that the statement that Paul uses about faith, hope and love, finishes with a paragraph that spells out in detail the love we can expect to find from a God who fills the roles of a father, husband, brother and friend. This passage is often used in marriages as it outlines the part love should play in the bride and groom's married life.

'Love is patient, love is kind. It does not envy, it does not boast, it is not proud. It is not rude, it is not self-seeking, it is not easily angered, it keeps no record of wrongs. Love does not delight in evil, but rejoices with the truth. It always hopes, always perseveres. Love never fails.' (1 Corinthians 13:4-8).

Well that would be true of the happy couple. Their vows would be based on their love and commitment and their hope for the future. We too can place ourselves in this dedicated position, when we desire to follow God.

What God says.

Why is faith so important to God? We could say using these comparisons that He wants us to know Him and know He loves us. This is the foundation of our faith. Amazingly, we go back again to Adam and Eve's relationship. We discussed before how when Adam and Eve chose to follow Satan and believe him and his word, above Father God's, that it broke their spiritual relationship. But now in our decision to refute the act made on our behalf, we choose to believe God's word over and above all else, based on our faith and love of Him.

Part of our faith in the relationships we have is that we believe what the person says. There's nothing more able to diminish your faith than finding out that what you've believed is either untrue or partially true. We have to believe in the people we care for, otherwise our partnership becomes a fissure of lies. God pronounces that He is the truth, to reassure us that He's not like that. He won't speak or act in ways that will deceive us and what He says is powerful in our lives when we trust Him.

'Consequently, faith comes from hearing the message and the message is heard through the Word of Christ.' (Romans 10:17).

Learning about Him as He speaks to us through His Word, the Bible, we're able to love Him more. The more we love Him, the more our faith grows. The more our love grows, the more we believe and trust what He tells us to be and do. It's a building exercise. As time goes on, we've a great hope for the work which God the Father, Jesus and the Holy Spirit are doing. As we trust Him more we align ourselves with who we really are, children of God - born again.

Did you ever play a game of trust with your dad, or big brother or someone with muscles, where you would fall backwards and trust they would catch you? Well, our heavenly Father is a bit like that. He says, "I won't take you anywhere I'm not able to prevent you from falling if you trust Me." What a relief it is when you feel those arms around you. You see Love, Faith and Hope are the only three things God asks us to bring to the table. He loved us first and has planned our marriage and life with Him down to the last detail. Now He only waits for us to fall in love with Him, believe in the future life with Him whatever it might bring, hope for tomorrow and ultimately eternity together.

What next?

Unfortunately, faith is something we have to exercise without knowing for sure the outcome. We use the best advice or information available, the best bank or investment, the best law for the problem, all sorts of topics which I'm sure you can think of, but so many of our solutions only lead us into larger problems and danger.

The Lord's Prayer contains important sentences, one of which is, 'lead us not into temptation, but deliver us from evil.' We need to know we've put our faith in the right place. It's a bit like having a gun with no bullet. Faith is the bullet you need to reach your target. But it's where you point the gun that makes the difference. When we have faith and trust in God we can be sure the target is a good one and He is the one who pulls the trigger. It's not that man is unable to make great moral and righteous decisions, but much as we try, we can't prevent the will and judgement of our own thinking to come adrift from God's perfect will. He never intended us to suffer the consequences of a world ruled by misunderstanding and weaknesses. Instead, he offers us the perfect way, if we'll trust Him.

Saving grace.

So where does faith come into all this for us? You might say that all religions call for faith, you'd be right of course. We exercise faith in those things that we make a religion for ourselves, even Atheism. However, Christian faith has its base belief in the 'unearned favour of God.' We probably understand this in terms of someone else being 'gracious' toward us when we make a mistake, or in rare situations when they forgive without any reference to something we've done against them. This is the grace of God and it's released as we choose to believe in His goodness toward us. We don't deserve

God's forgiveness. We can't make up for the things we've done wrong. If there was a charge made against us, how would we calculate what it should be? For Christians, faith begins and ends with the redemption of the cross and the resurrection leading to everlasting life. No other religion has such a central path of faith, where no law or legality can save us from sin, just the blood of Jesus shed for each one of us.

Faith and obedience.

The question is, do we want to obey or follow through the answers we receive through faith? For example, we're told of a great airline. However, we book with the cheapest because we want to save money and we're prepared to take the risk of a difficult journey. Or we're advised to use a certain bank but use another, only to find it crashes and we lose our investment. God responds to our faith but we still have the same free will to obey his advice or go our own way. Sometimes the advice we have from God isn't very comfortable to take and we have to use our utmost faith to be obedient. Through obedience, God can pour out His blessing and fulfil His purpose in our life, as we trust Him.

I have a confession, a behaviour which I certainly don't advise others to copy. When out with Roger, I often don't look when we cross the road. Holding his arm and probably chatting, (I'm always told I talk too much), I leave him to look each way and confidently step out when he does. While I'm not suggesting this is good practice, its a way to illustrate how we treat our faith in God.

When couples get married they don't have to jump through hoops that dictate what makes a good wife or husband. First and foremost they love each other. This will lead them to listen to their partners, serve them more willingly, give to them more generously and trust their judgement. I believe this is how our faith is grown. The Egyptians, Greeks and Romans etc. devised all sorts of practices to honour or appease their gods in the past. Their beliefs have centred around victory in battle, control of nature and sexual obligations. Now all these centuries later with all our knowledge and power of technology, we're still grappling with the same issues. Father God realised that His children couldn't comprehend the power of sin, just as our children don't recognise the dangers as they catapult themselves off the cliff into the sea below, 'believing' they can beat the odds and not be damaged. However, in Jesus, sin is met head on and the odds can be beaten if we have faith and belief.

Some years ago our family played host to a young Brazilian girl, Marcia, who was sixteen. Her faith was quite amazing in its purity. There was no pompous attitude about her, just a childlike faith and love. During her stay, I took her to visit a Bible study group for girls around her age. The conversation turned to current boyfriends and Marcia was encouraged to join in. Imagine the reaction from the group when Marcia said she only mixed with boys that her father had vetted. The room was electric. "Don't you mind?" they asked. "No", was the answer, "I trust my father. He knows who is best for me!" I think the other girls were secretly pleased they weren't Brazilian. But what a wonderful father to command the respect of his daughter like that. What a wise girl to trust her father and not rebel against him.

Signs and wonders.

'Jesus went throughout Galilee, teaching in their synagogues and preaching the good news of the kingdom,

healing every kind of disease and sickness among the people.' (Matthew 4:23).

Did your Mum have a favourite saying? Mine had two. One was, "Is nothing sacred?", which she quoted when she had enough of us kids encroaching on her space. The other was, her most favourite, "Deeds, not words," her school motto. It had obviously been the principle with the greatest impact on her. She passed it on with great conviction. You can have a great orator, philosopher and intellectual, but what they say won't hold water for long if it isn't backed up with action. Jesus preached about the kingdom of heaven, but He was also illustrating his message by miraculous works. He told His disciples that they too should walk in His example, as they would do greater works that He himself, if they believed! John Wimber was a great man of God. He'd been part of an American pop band in the early sixties called 'The Paramours', but decided instead to follow Jesus. In his search for the truth about God he read the Bible and subsequently went along to a church. At the end of the service as everyone was on their way home, he stopped the minister and asked, "When do you do the stuff?" "The stuff?" the minister replied. "You know", said John, "the healing and miracles."

You might think that John's question was somewhat naive but it always gets me thinking – why don't we see healing and miracles happen if we have faith to believe in Jesus? It's only my opinion, but I have always thought that our way of life impinges on our ability to be uncompromising in our faith for the greater things of God. In less westernised parts of the world miracles of healing etc. are seen more often.

A lovely lady, who used to be part of our youth group years ago, came to visit us. She was a nurse in cardiac intensive care units, but she has worked for many years now on the mercy ships which anchor around the coast of Africa. These ships offer surgery to the local people in the countries they stop at. She told us of the wonderful things that the staff had seen God doing for their patients in answer to their prayers. We discussed this at length and came to the conclusion that those dear brothers and sisters had truly given up their lives in faith. They lived in an atmosphere of prayer and compassion, making the ship their home for sometimes years and only wished to have God's good pleasure as their form of pay. No wonder they experienced, as Jesus had promised, His Holy Spirit healing the sick and setting captives free. With faith we all have the capacity to see great things happen. The more we love and believe in all that God says, the more the door to the supernatural world opens.

Another example is a team from our local churches who came back from The Gambia with stories of amazing works of healing they saw when they prayed in Jesus' name for the sick villagers they met. These illnesses were extreme, and they were amazed at the healing they saw take place before their eyes. Why then, don't we see the same results of our prayers? I think there are two reasons. The first is the lack of education. Now that sounds like a wild statement but with our educated western hat on we've a whole raft of information about any ailment we can almost unwittingly line up against the power of pure faith. The second reason is that these people are surrounded with spiritual awareness, which causes them to respond to the prayer of faith with a simple belief.

'And He said, "I tell you the truth, unless you change and become like little children, you will never enter the kingdom of heaven." (Matthew 18:3).

Jesus says we should be humble like children. When you think about a child, with their reliance on adult carers and faith for safety in their hands, you can make the comparison to our 'slightly' conceited attitude to our knowledge of the situation. This, of course, wipes out or at least diminishes our faith.

"'If you have faith in God," Jesus answered, "Truely I tell you, if anyone says to this mountain, 'Go throw yourself into the sea,' and does not doubt in his heart but believes that what he says will happen, it will be done for him. Therefore I tell you, whatever you ask for in prayer, believe that you have received it and it will be yours.'" (Mark 11:22-24).

Does all of this sound outlandish? Maybe so, but there's a saying, that you start your understanding by taking a leap of faith. You put your apprehension and fear aside and, as if faced with a leap across a ravine, you keep your gaze fixed on what is in front of you. That's the person of Jesus. As you leap, He holds out His arms to catch you. Nothing can please Him more than your trust in Him. His love is unconditional, so you can make that jump just as you are. He'll be the one who fills all the blank spaces with understanding and faith.

To believe, or not to believe? That is the question.

If we wanted to find an illustration of faith, there is no better example than the Bible itself. There are many references of great deeds of faith, but in John 20:19-29 we find an account of the doubt and belief of Thomas, a disciple of Jesus.

Thomas, like us, so often needed proof of what he was expected to believe. Very wise! He was not a man unwilling to take risks when the need presented itself. His love for Jesus was not in question. In fact it was he who encouraged the others to go with Jesus to Bethany when they heard of the death of Lazarus. This was dangerous as many of the establishment where seeking to kill Him. However, as the story unfolds, Thomas was not around when the women and disciples found the tomb empty, with Jesus risen. He did not see the angels or indeed Jesus Himself when He appeared first to Mary and then to the disciples as they gathered in the locked upper room where He showed them His wounded hands, feet and side.

When the disciples told Thomas, his reaction was probably quite reasonably doubtful. When faced with this joyful group, who had after all been through an unprecedented trauma at the death of Jesus, he was not in the mood to believe. Thomas epitomises our reaction when presented with a spiritual phenomenon. He wanted proof and stated clearly that there was no way that he would believe that Christ had risen unless he could put his hands into His wounds!

When we are presented with supernatural events we revert to our natural reaction to the unfamiliar and when others wish to share with us the experiences they have had in their Christian walk we stubbornly disbelieve, even turn away. The Lord Jesus though, full of grace, understood the mind of Thomas and so obliged his scepticism by appearing when he was part of the gathering. He offered him the proof he wanted by saying, "Reach out your hand and put your finger in My hand and your hand in My side." How amazed Thomas must have been at the love of his master who wanted him to know first hand this wonderful truth.

As we call out to Jesus and ask Him to help our unbelief, He returns our prayer with our own personal experience of His presence. However, if we turn away, block our ears and stubbornly disbelieve we miss all the wonder of God's marvellous grace.

Through the crucifixion our sins are forgiven and through the resurrection we too share in life after death, our spirit joining Jesus in life everlasting. Can we risk not taking the risk?

Even with all of this we are left with questions.

I believe in God and I pray, but more often than not He doesn't answer my prayers, so I've stopped bothering.

It can be difficult sometimes when our prayers are somehow held up and we don't receive the answer we want or expect. God always gives us the right answer and although it may not seem so at the time, His answer will key into the well-being or success or our future. Like a friend of mine who prayed and prayed that God would find a lovely man for her to marry. After years, she has now married a man who is exactly right for her and both are ecstatically happy. Or a girl I knew who, really believing in God, prayed that her husband would be healed. Unfortunately, he died, but she felt the presence of God even more keenly and He provided for her in miraculous ways. Sometimes we don't pray for the right things. Like children who ask for things that maybe all their friends have. However, as loving parents we know those things won't be right for them. It's hard to disappoint our children but our desire for their well-being overrides giving in to their demands. Very often our prayers are for those who are ill and we don't see their release. We just have to trust that God will turn the circumstance to good in some way and although sometimes terribly painful, He does. Please don't give up praying, as God's timing isn't ours and He loves to know that you trust Him.

I made a leap of faith but nothing in my life has changed.

When you're first married it can seem like nothing has changed even when everything has changed. The most important thing has stayed the same, your love for each other. However, you've embarked on an adventure together and the whole world, as it were, is waiting for you to explore it. Jesus told us to ask and it will be given to us, to knock and the door will be opened, seek and we will find. But remember the most important thing is to love.

PART THREE

THE HOME STRAIGHT

Home sweet home.

In 1982 we decided that we would leave our adopted home of Australia and return to the U.K. It wasn't that we were unhappy. We had a great life with wonderful friends. But after a trip to dear 'Old Blighty' we knew this is where we were supposed to be.

I've heard Australians say that as they came into a port in Australia the smell of the Gum trees filled them with joy at being 'home.' Likewise for us, flying in over the patchwork scenery of the English countryside we could hardly contain ourselves with the happiness of coming back to where we knew we belonged.

After spending sixteen years in the country of our choice, what was it that made us feel so overjoyed to return? There are many English people who live abroad who would never want to come back and would in fact think that those who do, have lost the plot. But for us, it was a very different experience, one I'd like to use as an example in this chapter.

As you can imagine, the Israel that Jesus lived in was oppressed. The Israelites had always had to fight for their identity and they lived with a mixture of dread and hope. Now with Roman rule and harsh religious oversight it seemed that nothing would ever change. Then suddenly this young man came on the scene. He was no ordinary preacher, of whom there were many, He preached a different message. One in which He spoke of the 'Kingdom of God.' If our ears pricked up when others spoke of England after a trip to the U.K., how much would theirs be open to the message of Israel as a kingdom once again, as in the days of David the great godly king.

So the people listened as Jesus told them stories to explain this mysterious kingdom and what it should mean to them. However, He didn't speak about patchwork fields and swallows, Gum trees or Koala Bears. Instead He spoke of the upside down culture of this place and how you might enter it, almost like Alice in Wonderland as she followed the white rabbit into a hidden different world.

How can I explain why I love England so much? It couldn't be that the weather was better, nor the people. The culture is roughly the same. Yes the scenery was magnificent, but that wasn't it either. So what was I hankering for? Well pure and simple, it's where I belonged. Just as the world of which Jesus spoke of was where He belonged. I'm sure His listeners would have been confused, curious and excited by this new kingdom that God oversees.

The Kingdom of God.

Matthew recalls the teaching, starting with the 'Sermon on the mount.'

'Blessed (Congratulations) to those who are poor in spirit, for yours is the Kingdom of God.' (Matthew 5:3).

They must have wondered what He meant. Maybe if you're poor and don't surround yourselves with the encumbrance of material things, you'll find you'll be welcomed into this promised Kingdom and be blessed. Or did it mean that if you're not puffed up with religious 'does and don'ts' you'll be welcomed in? Either way it sounds as though you can be yourself without any trappings! Jesus went on to say,

'Blessed (Congratulations) to those who mourn, for they will be comforted.' (Matthew 5:4).

But how can you congratulate someone for mourning? Maybe it meant mourning for something else – peace, joy, love or even righteousness. Or maybe to mourn for those who've lost their way. Whatever He meant, it seemed their wishes would come true in the Kingdom of God! Jesus went on, spelling out how their behaviour would have to be in this special place.

When we began to live a normal life back in the U.K., things that were the same seemed different. It wasn't that we swapped our flip flops, (thongs in Australia) for wellie boots, but more that the same things had a different slant. Jesus started unpacking how this worked in the Kingdom. Nothing would change. All the laws that Moses received from God the Father, would stand right into heaven itself. Those who listened knew the laws well, their culture was built around them. However, there would be an important change in the way they were perceived and this had to do with the heart it came from. Adultery for instance would be seen not just from the act itself but from everything that pertained to it. Assassination of your brother's character and spirit was as serious as murdering his flesh. What was this all about? Was Jesus saying don't commit adultery or flirt with immorality because it will harm you and others. Also, please don't speak unkindly about others as God hates criticism.

When a woman who was caught in adultery was brought to Jesus and was asked to respond to her behaviour, He said,

"'If any one of you is without sin, let him be the first to throw a stone at her." At this those who heard began to go away one at a time, the older ones first, until only Jesus was left, with the woman still standing there. "Woman, where are they? Has no-one condemned you?" "No one, Sir," she said. "Then neither do I condemn you," Jesus declared, "Go now and leave your life of sin." (John 8:1-11).

He has compassion and love for all who are trapped in sin.

The way in.

Jesus taught how repentance and faith would be the requirement to enter into the Kingdom of God. He spelt out those things that would hinder us, not because there was any entry check, but that certain kinds of conduct, even in our thinking, would hold us back from being welcomed in. Hindrances, like riches being more important than people, revenge instead of peace and indifference rather than mercy.

In fact, all things that are more important to us, than loving God and treating others just as we would ourselves. Some people may have thought, 'Sounds good but just wait until I've built up my business, finished my present fling and generally got my head in the right place, then I'll definitely give it a go.'

Jesus said, "Listen, you are in danger of building your happiness on something that can be washed away in a second. I am the king of the Kingdom and unless you build your life on Me you will not be able to be where I am."

The King.

Every kingdom has to have a sovereign, after all, that's what makes it a kingdom. In days of old, the monarch made the laws. He would be active in policies which affected his people, not only for land and taxes etc. but in the battles that were fought on behalf of the kingdom. We're not used to this sort of leadership from modern day monarchs but this is in essence the kingship that Jesus brings. Obviously, if the reign brought hardship and injustice, the subjects were under obligation to follow. But if there was righteousness of rule and a willingness of the monarch to serve his people even unto death, then those who were his subjects were also ready to give up their lives to follow and obey. After all, this King didn't demand heavy duties from his subjects, that left them in bondage, poor and disrespected. He reassured them that He'd never desert them.

'Come to me all you who are weary and burdened, and I will give you rest. Take my yoke upon you and learn from me, for I am gentle and humble in heart and you will find rest for your souls. For my yoke is easy and my burden is light.' (Matthew 11:28-30).

When the king is near, he brings with him the knowledge and reality of his kingdom. So it was with Jesus. Whenever He was near, the Kingdom and all that it signified would break through to this world. However, Jesus went even further, to say that the Kingdom was in us. What could He have meant by that? Well, just as we carry the knowledge of who we are and where we come from, when we belong to Jesus, we carry His DNA and the characteristics and the nationality of the Kingdom. Kind of like a passport that has been stamped and verified by the Holy Spirit. Even so, it's our behaviour, our attitude and perspective that reflect where we belong.

Let's face it though, it won't be easy. Jesus warned us that we're not of this world and frankly others won't understand us. But that doesn't mean we can't enjoy all the blessings and power of the family of God and His righteous Kingdom.

Heaven on earth.

Like other Christian families, we like to spend time each spring and summer attending Christian camps and conventions. It's something I would have thought in the past as being the most boring and frightening 'holiday' ever. The strange thing is that on the whole everyone who attends these events seems happy. Equally there are thousands of people who regularly go to festivals, often wallowing in mud up to their arm pits, who are also happy. But there's a difference. At Christian conventions, apart from times of wonderful music and worship to God, people are expected to interact with others. Often those attending will be asked in the seminars to break into groups made up with people they don't know and then discuss some deep and meaningful subject that concerns us all. It's quite interesting to find you're paired up with a Bishop's wife or someone quite intimidating, only to find they're as vulnerable as you and come away feeling as though you have made a friend for life. Most don't smoke or drink, so that's a no-no, and there's an air of love which you've never come across before. This Christian stuff is definitely a different kind of experience.

Another thing about these events is that everyone is so polite, helping wherever they can. Ushering you into the queue ahead of them, which is handy if you really need the loo! Lost property is bursting at the seams with all sorts of things from purses to combs! So if you're forgetful you can be sure that even your pen will be taken to the 'lost property'. Children are safe without their parents, and there's no swearing or coarse language. Little by little, all your tension, worry and stress of it all, fades away and you relax like never before. You just don't want to go home. Could this be like the Kingdom of God?

The King is here and He's doing some extraordinary things. People are being released from all sorts of difficulties, fear, sadness and emotional upsets. Others are being healed and certainly there's a great presence of peace and joy. It could be the general high that those crazy Christians are feeling as they leave to go, but they still feel ten feet tall and start acting as though they're much more clear about who they are, and where they belong.

'The Kingdom of God is like a mustard seed, which a man took and planted in his field. Though it is the smallest of all your seeds, yet when it grows, it is the largest of garden plants and becomes a tree, so that the birds of the air come and perch in its branches.' (Matthew 13:31-32).

I love this parable. In fact I have a picture that was painted for me of a tree which gave every type of bird a place to call their home. This explains the Kingdom. Although it starts in the centre of our hearts as a little seed of faith, as we're watered by God's love, our roots go down and we grow to bring a place where others can rest and find Jesus.

It says in the gospels that Jesus came preaching the good news of the Kingdom, telling people to repent and healing them. They must have thought, 'How do we find this Kingdom?' 'Do you have to go up to heaven, or be very good?' Jesus' reply was, "Seek and you will find, knock and the door will be opened for you."

Finding the treasure.

'The Kingdom of Heaven is like a treasure hidden in the field. When a man found it, he hid it again, and then in his joy went and sold all he had and bought that field.' (Matthew 13:44).

Will we take part in all the good it offers us, just as Jesus said? Will we pray that God will supply us with all that we need on our part to make this happen, both physically and spiritually? Will we ask God to forgive us our sins, those we know of and those we don't and give us the grace to forgive in the same way He forgives us? Will we ask that God will lead us away from the things that tempt us, so we don't do the things that He disapproves of, and be delivered from all sorts of evil?

Jesus said, "Go and tell everyone else about this." Will we tell them how precious the truth of this Kingdom is? So precious that others have turned their back on everything they had, or found to be of worth, to exchange it for this great treasure. Will we pray that God's name will be called Our Father, Daddy, and tell them how wonderful He is? Will we pray that His Kingdom will come soon? Not any earthly kingdom, where things go horribly wrong, but the Kingdom of Righteousness.

His is the 'Kingdom', the power, and the glory for ever and ever.

Even with all of this we are left with questions.

It's all very well talking about a kingdom, but we already live in a kingdom and so there are things we have to obey. How does that work?

Well, Jesus was asked a very similar question and He answered it like this:- *"Give to Caesar what is Caesar's and to God what is God's." (Matthew 22:21)*. In other words, you have to obey the law of the land whilst living as a citizen of God's Kingdom.

Where is this kingdom? What's it like?

Jesus speaks of it as a real place:- *'Then the King will say to those on His right. Come, you who are blessed by My Father, take your inheritance, the Kingdom prepared for you since the creation of the world.' (Matthew 25:34).* Also:- *'Do not let your hearts be troubled. Trust in God; trust also in me. In my Father's house there are many rooms; if it were not so I would have told you. I am going there to prepare a place for you. I will come back to take you with Me that you should also be where I am. You know the way to the place where I am going.' (John 14:1-4).*

The Kingdom exists now, just as England existed when I was in Australia. I may have lived on the other side of the Earth but I had a British passport, accent, family and heritage and I have the choice to live even if abroad, as a British woman. Likewise, we may live here on Earth but we're actually citizens of God and members of God's household. I am sure if Jesus has prepared it, we'll find it just perfect.

LAST BUT NOT LEAST

Church.

It would seem obvious that if you want to know anything about God the place most likely to have all the information you need would be church on a Sunday morning. After all, this is where those who profess Christian beliefs will be found and the services called worship are carried out there. Even so, when exploring what Christianity could offer you, going to church can be quite confusing and maybe even off-putting. It certainly was for me. I was always afraid that someone would jump out and somehow involve me in something I didn't want to do. So, it will be helpful to look at some practices you might encounter and how they fit in to our theme of relationship and righteousness.

To many, church signifies the ancient buildings we see scattered throughout our cities, towns and villages. They link us to our historic past. Also to many, the only times they venture across the threshold for any kind of spiritual input is for marriages, funerals and christenings. Just the smell of them can be off-putting. It's a bit like going to the doctors surgery where everyone whispers, even if they're not talking about their health. Once inside the church, we feel we must be reverent but we actually don't know how to do that.

Church isn't about buildings, it's about the assembly of like minded people. A congregation who gather to share their faith and make the way 'church' is done, more real and relaxed. Children are welcome and you don't have to feel that you need to sit by the door to make a fast retreat if they play up. The differences in the way church is done can cause us to doubt their validity. This concerned me too until I began to recognise that relationship takes in a variety of differences without compromising the depth of closeness and care. If you asked those who go to church, what denomination they are, I'm sure you'd find a diverse and yet united bunch of people.

My children differ in all sorts of ways. The way they express themselves, their interests etc., so it's sensible to think that groups of Christians will prefer to practice different expressions of their religious beliefs. What's essential though is that they're all united in believing that Jesus is their Saviour and it's through faith in the redemption of the cross and that they've been restored by grace to share in eternity with Him. It's such a shame when the type of service overpowers the important relational occasion that attending church is intended to be, especially when the Lord only cares about whether you're there.

Church really is home. It's where we go to meet with our family. At the time of the first church the apostles, disciples and followers of Jesus would meet in their homes. Churches didn't exist. It's true that there were synagogues where Jews assembled for their form of worship, but unfortunately Christians weren't welcome there. Christians became a community, a family, where they shared not only their love and worship of Jesus, God the Father and Holy Spirit, but also they loved and shared with each other and the community.

There is nothing I love more than to have my children and their families come to visit our home. Unfortunately, families rarely stay in the same vicinity of each other these days, which makes reunion all the more precious. Not so long ago it would be the custom to meet up at the parental home once a week or as often as possible. When my kids get together, apart from catching up on the family news, they spend time laughing about some memory or other, those things that link them together. I believe that is how church should be. We go to church to see our Dad and to be with our family. Those practices we keep during the service all have some reference to the connection with the family life of the church, and the essentials of our faith and God's Word.

'They devoted themselves to the apostles teaching and to the fellowship, to the breaking of bread and to prayer. Everyone was filled with awe, and many wonders and miraculous signs were done by the apostles. All the believers were together and had everything in common. Selling their possessions and goods, they gave to anyone as he had need. Every day they continued to meet together in the temple courts. They broke bread, in their homes and ate together with glad and sincere hearts, praising God and enjoying the favour of all the people. And the Lord added to their number daily those who were being saved.' (Acts 2:42-47).

Loving and learning.

Worship can be interpreted in many ways, but I love the interpretation that comes from the Greek word 'proskuneo', which means come together to kiss. That's exactly what happens, I believe, when we sing our love songs, hymns and choruses to God. We come to our Father and kiss Him, just the same as we would to our earthly Dad. There are other references and explanations of worship such as, 'reverence with awe.' This we do when we praise God through our singing and prayer. There are also references to 'showing honour.' In the same way when families get together they honour their parents.

When my children, now adults themselves, share their worries and joys with me, often asking advice, I'm happy to listen and help where I can. This forms a great bond between us as we walk together through whatever the situation calls for. I believe prayer to be like this – an opportunity to thank God for all that is good, but bringing our worries to Him too.

We have so much to thank God for and when we read the scriptures together, they re-establish those principles on which we place our trust and faith. There's also always a time to bring our concern for others to our Father's attention and the natural thing to do is to discuss and pray for those who most need it. It's a powerful thought that all through the country and indeed the world, other members of our Christian family are praying too.

As well as this, God talks about worship being an act of service. Not just words but actually doing the stuff. Because prayer is imperative, we can often ignore the fact we can be the answer to our own prayers. You'll find church is a place where this army of ordinary people can be involved in all sorts of community projects, showing the love of God not only in, but through, the church.

I remember a story of a young man who went to a group of elders at the church to complain. He had taken in a homeless man to stay with him, but was upset that the church wasn't doing anything about it. The elders' response was to point out that he himself was the 'church' so the need was in fact being met by the body of the church.

Why the need to confess?

I remember an embarrassing moment in my past when, as a school girl, we'd be marched off to the local church to confess our sins. I wouldn't be able to remember anything I'd done that was sinful, so I used to make them up. Imagine how embarrassed I was on one occasion, to see all my classmates on coming out of the confessional, with their fingers in their ears as I had talked too loudly. I wonder what they made of my made up sin!

Do you have someone you can off-load to? All those things we pick up in a week can spoil who we really are, even if we're not really aware of anything sinful. The things we say and others say to us, that can often feel liked a barb in the heart and aren't easily forgotten, or things that make us cross and aren't resolved. Roger once explained it to our youth group as, putting on a clean white T-shirt which becomes grubby and stained by all those little things we do, or others do to us without even really noticing it. The time in church when we ask God either to forgive us, or to give us the grace to forgive someone else, is like giving our grubby T-shirt to the Lord and graciously He gives us one back that's been freshly laundered.

To admit you're wrong to someone is a commendable act which takes humility and it also takes strength of character to forgive. These acts of repentance and forgiveness bring reconciliation and peace for members of the church. They are acts which through our time together, and with Jesus, renew our strength and relationships.

'If we claim to be without sin, we deceive ourselves and the truth is not in us. If we confess our sins, He is faithful and just and will forgive us our sins, and purify us from all unrighteousness. If we claim we have not sinned, we make Him out to be a liar, and His Word has no place in our lives.' (1 John 1:8-10).

A shared meal. Why communion?

When my family is all together we always share a meal. It's round the table that we all come again as a family to talk and laugh. It's usually me that prepares it, but I really don't mind, as having them part of my day again is worth all the effort. I'm able to give myself once more to my children and their little ones and now even their little ones! Each time we share communion we share that which Jesus has prepared for us.

Jesus said to His disciples, those who were to Him like children, *"I have eagerly desired to eat this Passover with you before I suffer"* (Luke 22:15). He desired this special meal to herald a time that He would, by His suffering and death, break the bondage that mankind was under, the rule of Satan. He knew full well what lay ahead of Him, as it was laid out in many places in scripture, but Isaiah said that 'He had set His face like flint and wouldn't be ashamed at the task.' And so there He was, our dear Lord, only hinting at what lay before the poor disciples who would have to bear the terrible loss of their Master, who was willing to make the ultimate sacrifice for those He came to save – you and me.

He took the bread, offered it up to God and said, *"This is my body which is given for you, do this in remembrance of Me" (Luke 22:19)*. Then later He took the cup of wine, offered it to God the Father and said, *"This cup is the new covenant in my blood which is poured out for you" (Luke 22:20)*. He'd prepared Himself and He told His disciples and us, that we were to remember the significance of this at a meal shared together.

It would be great to know that when my children meet after my death and shared a meal together they could say to each other, "Do you remember when Mum..." I'm sure the disciples did exactly that: "Do you remember when Jesus fed the five thousand?" or "how about when He walked on water?" or "how we all cried with joy when He healed the sick." More than that though, they would remind each other, and now us, of our beloved, Redeemer and Messiah as He prepared to give His life for our freedom.

When we share communion we don't just think of the cross, although that's the most central part of our faith, but we remember the life of Jesus too. Who He was and is, our dearest Lord, our hero and our Saviour. We think of what He has done and is doing for us, personally and corporately. We remember what He taught us, and how we now belong in the family of God because of His sacrifice.

The promise.

Even with all of this, it does seem a bit strange to be re-enacting a meal by taking bread and wine as a symbol of Christ's body and blood. What was the real reason for this 'Passover' meal that Jesus shared with His friends? What was so special?

To the Jews, celebrating their holy days is of the utmost importance. God told them to remember on these days just how He had rescued them from complete obliteration. So they celebrate with symbols which help them remember, honour and thank God. By far the most important feast is the Passover. It's the day that is set aside for the people of God to remember their flight from Egypt and how God delivered them from the hands of their enemy by separating the water of the Red Sea. Practising Jews still keep their Passover and set out the meal just as they were told to by God way back in the time of Moses. Christians too join together on the Thursday before Easter to remember the last supper, which is the Passover, to remember all that was said and done that evening.

Symbols play a big part in the human psyche. We can all immediately identify with an emblem or symbol that identifies something special or particularly important to us. A football team's crest, the Olympic rings, or in Christianity – the cross or a dove.

God had entered into a covenant with Abraham right at the beginning of the story of God's people. A covenant, or legal agreement, is usually made as an exchange by two participating parties. However, in this covenant the major party is far superior than the other, and all the responsibility to provide the benefits of the covenant fall on His shoulders. The only proviso is the acceptance of the other party to the terms and conditions.

Of course God was the major contributor in this covenant and at various times He told His people to put in place symbols or symbolic acts which would remind them of His commitment to them and their part in it all. Rather like the anniversaries we keep to remind us of our weddings. A wedding being a good example of the sort of covenant I've described. I love weddings. I almost always cry and think the service is over too quickly for the size of the commitment the couple are taking. When we get 'married' we do so based purely on love and trust. None of us really know how our lives might pan out. In the service, the men and women promise to love, cherish and honour, and for the woman once upon a time, obey. These promises follow the same outline as the covenant God made with Israel and later through Jesus with us. The bride and groom pledge to share their lives and wealth and stay true to each till death parts them. They promise that even though times may get tough, they'll be there for each other.

God also gives to us His protection and shares His life with us, staying true to us in all situations. Wedding rings signify eternal life. As the rings are exchanged, so too are the lives of the bride and groom. They become one with each other. Having done this they officially sign the register when the wife then takes her husband's name as her own, just as we do when we become Christians. Then onto the celebrations, where in that special meal the couple share the bread (wedding cake) and wine, declaring their marriage at 'their' wedding feast. This is the depth of the covenant we enter into with Jesus when we give our lives to Him. It's a wonderful time and all the guests join in the happiness that the bride and groom have, sending them off joyfully into their life together.

Could this be us, remembering again as we take communion that Jesus was fulfilling God's promise to us? Actually this is a seal on that first promise God made to Moses, to set the people free. You know those very important documents that have a scarlet wax seal. Well our seal is the blood of Jesus, authentication and making available the promises made centuries before. This was the 'Old Covenant', and Jesus declared He is the 'New Covenant.' It would be through Him and through His blood and none other, that we would be forgiven and set free. This is why we celebrate communion, we remember our freedom, we remember the agony of the cross, but we also remember our Husband and our marriage to Him, and how much He loves us.

The Preach.

We couldn't end the chapter about church without including something on preaching! I have to admit I've been guilty of being bored by certain ways that a few preachers and teachers have expounded on scripture to enlighten their congregation. It reminds me of the story of a father and his young son in a church service. After what seemed an extraordinarily long time, the boy looks around and spots a plaque. He whispers to his dad, "What are all those names for?" "Those are the names of all the people who died in the services," replies his father. "What?" said the boy in horror. "Did they all die from boredom?"

We've talked about the Word of God as being like a love letter; a way we build our faith when we hear the voice of God speaking right into our lives. Hearing certain scriptures unravelled and looked into, can help us view the Bible with new eyes.

Years ago a friend of ours brought his non believing wife to a service. During the talk she became more and more agitated and couldn't wait to leave. She thought her husband had spoken to the minister and accused him of revealing intimate details about her life. He hadn't and no one else knew anything about her. It was the Word of God that spoke directly into who she was. You may be pleased to know this isn't usual. God had a special place for her to work in His kingdom. For many years now she and her husband have been missionaries in remote parts of the world.

Through what we learn and how God speaks to us through scripture, He can become far more than a voice from the sky or a set of rules we try to obey. He 'gets you' and knows you more than you know yourself.

Hearing or reading the Word of God is like eating. We need to eat to receive strength for our body, in the same way we need to eat the scriptures to strengthen our spiritual self. Unfortunately, we can soon become spiritually anorexic, so when something that isn't right comes along, we don't have the strength to fight back and we fall. Of course we wouldn't dream of only eating once a week, so why leave it up to the poor old preacher to supply all our spiritual needs on Sunday? No, we need to look at the Bible as much as we can. But much like food, the more of the Bible we consume, the more we want.

There are many good Bible aids to help you think about what you've read. However, I think the best way is to be a bit of a gourmet. Take little tastes and take a long time to chew it over. That way you'll hear a small but powerful voice speak into your heart in a personal way.

'All Scripture is God breathed and is useful for teaching, rebuking, correcting and training in righteousness, so that the servant of God may be thoroughly equipped for every good work.' (2 Timothy 3:16-17).

What more could you want?

Most churches have small groups to join. It's a great way to make friends and get to know what makes these people tick. I hope like me you'll take the chance and go with an open heart and mind to see for yourself.

Even with all of this we are left with questions.

Do you have to be committed to one church or become a member?

Certainly in my experience you don't. However, there maybe some churches which still like you to become a member if you attend regularly. Personally I can't see what difference it makes. Perhaps they want to know that you're committed to that church if you take up more responsible positions. It would be unusual though.

Can you take communion without being a committed Christian?

We've discussed the meaning of communion and why we practice 'bread and wine.' It's similar to the practice of remembering our wedding anniversaries. If you haven't been married to the person you wouldn't be able to celebrate the wedding. However, if you believe in Jesus and that He died to save us from our sins that's fulfilling the reason Jesus died for you and you'd be welcome to receive the sacrament.

THE CONCLUSION

The new me!

I couldn't finish this book without at least having some reference to a phrase we all know, 'being born again.' We've had all sorts of topics using these words as their slogan, but rarely is this important statement spelt out fully to those who really don't understand the meaning. One such man was called Nicodemus. He was no ordinary man though. He was a high ranking Pharisee, someone who was learned and wise.

Like other Pharisees he'd been listening and watching Jesus very carefully, but rather than criticising, he acknowledged Jesus as being someone special. He couldn't quite work out what was going on, so was drawn to find out. He went secretly, at night, to find out more. We can be like that, can't we?

I was brought up knowing about God, but when I turned away from Him completely, I longed to find Him again. The last place I thought of going was to church, with all those pious people, so I pulled any passing evangelists who knocked on my door in by their ties. It didn't matter what their preferred religion was, I just wanted to hear more! Do you know what I mean? Well Nicodemus would certainly have understood how I felt.

Jesus didn't try to engage him in discussion about scripture, Nicodemus knew all that. Instead Jesus said something much more radical. He said, "*unless you are born again you won't understand what I am telling you.*" Naturally, Nicodemus pushed Him on the subject. "*How on earth can that be, who can be born again when they are fully grown?*" "*I am telling you the truth,*" Jesus said, "*Unless you are born of water and of the Spirit you cannot enter the kingdom of God. Flesh gives birth to the flesh, but the Holy Spirit gives birth to the spirit.*"

Still Nicodemus was puzzled, he must have understood that babies were born in human form, but the Holy Spirit was the giver of the life in the spirit, but how did that happen? "*Why are you so surprised,*" asked Jesus, "*You don't see the wind, but you see what it is doing. No-one can ever come into the presence of God except those that come from God. Moses lifted up the bronze serpent in the desert so people believed in their healing. God has given His only Son that He might be lifted up so that all who believe in Him might be saved.*" (John 3:3-16 paraphrased).

If I was in Nicodemus' shoes I don't know that I would have understood either. But somehow God in His grace to me, led me through all my misunderstandings. All I really knew was that I wanted to believe in Him, did believe in Him and all He had done. Of course, now I understand the whole meaning of 'choosing' to belong to God. In doing so it's as if we're taken back to the beginning. We start our lives once more, knowing God as our Father and being connected fully to Him by the Spirit. Strangely, we are like children when first start out on our new Christian life.

'Like new born babes, crave pure spiritual milk so that by it you grow up in your salvation.' (1 Peter 2:2).

As a mother loves her new-born just as much as her other children, from the moment we are 'born again,' Jesus loves us as His children. Nicodemus must have got it though, as he's mentioned again by John, defending Jesus at His trial and later bringing gifts to anoint Christ's body after the crucifixion.

I'm sure, like me, you've come across others who've had amazing training and teaching on the subject of their choice, but don't fully understand how things work. Their intellectual ability doesn't seem to help them when putting that knowledge into practice, while others have a natural aptitude for the subject in hand. Spiritually, we're a bit like that. We can learn scripture, cross every 't' and dot every 'i' but still not actually understand the working of it. Only when we abandon our own intellect and place ourselves at the feet of Jesus, can the Holy Spirit fill in all the gaps. As Christians, one of the hardest things is to disengage ourselves from outcomes and concentrate more on building our relationship with our heavenly family; Father, Son and Holy Spirit. It's just a question of choice!

Baptism

When Jesus describes how we are 'born again,' as well as mentioning the Holy Spirit, He also mentions water. We all know water is cleansing, as indeed that is what it does. Right from the beginning of the gospels we hear about John the Baptist preaching to the people that they should repent and be baptised. Baptism wasn't a new idea for the Jews. They understood by immersing themselves, they declared a complete change. You've heard of the baptism of fire, which has the same inference, a complete, overpowering and transforming experience. The symbolism in being completely immersed signifies our death, in this case to sin, and our subsequent rising out of the water to new birth.

Jesus Himself was baptised at the beginning of His ministry. Not that He needed to be. But through this act He showed obedience to His Father, remembering that He too was human. Just as for us, Jesus was publicly declaring the death of His own flesh and a complete dedication to the life God the Father had destined for Him. Father God then affirmed Jesus in an audible voice, *"This is my Son whom I love; with Him I am well pleased."* (Matthew 3:17).

For us Christians this is a special moment too. As we go down under the water we make a statement of faith, that our sins are forgiven and we've started a new life in the Spirit. It's a seal, a covenant, on our commitment to Him. A public acknowledgement to those, here on earth, and those in heaven, of who we are and to whom we belong. We may not hear the Father's voice audibly, but we hear it in our heart. This is the only conclusion we ever need to make. Why? Because it supersedes all others and makes sense of our lives here and right on into eternity.

We all have our own journey, and circumstances, and our experiences have a bearing on our perception and attitude to life. However we have all come from the same source and are of great value to God, a value worth dying for!

The Prodigal Son

'There was a man who had two sons. The younger one said to his father, "Father, give me my share of the estate." So he divided his property between them.
Not long after that, the younger son got together all he had, set off for a distant country and there squandered his wealth in wild living. After he had spent everything, there was a severe famine in the whole country, and he began to be in need. So he went and hired himself out to a citizen of that country, who sent him to the fields to feed the pigs. He longed to fill his stomach with the pods the pigs were eating, but no one gave him anything.
When he came to his senses, he said, "How many of my father's hired men have food to spare, and here I am starving to death! I will set out and go back to my father and say to him, "Father, I have sinned against heaven and against you. I am no longer worthy to be called your son; make me like one of your hired men.""" So he got up and went to his father.

But while he was still a long way off, his father saw him and was filled with compassion for him; he ran to his son, threw his arms around him and kissed him. The son said to him, "Father, I have sinned against heaven and against you. I am no longer worthy to be called your son." But the father said to his servants, "Quick! Bring the best robe and put it on him. Put a ring on his finger and sandals on his feet. Bring the fatten calf and kill it. Let's have a feast and celebrate. For this son of mine was dead but is alive again; he was lost and is found." So they began to celebrate.' (Luke 15:11-24).

How do I make the step of being born again?

Pray, out loud, a simple prayer.

"Jesus, I believe you're my Saviour and died to forgive me of my sins, paying the price on the cross. I repent of all I have done wrong, both those things I know of and those that I don't. Please will you come with Your Spirit and become the Lord of my life, that I might follow you forever. Amen."

ABOUT THE AUTHOR

Jill is a mother of four and lives with her husband in North Devon. A Christian of thirty eight years, she has been actively involved in youth work and together with her husband Roger founded a home for homeless adults with whom they lived for some years, sharing the ups and downs of community life. Jill's real passion is to communicate to others, in an easy manner, the life changing relationship we have with the God-head. Enabling them to meet with Jesus in a way that relates to the times they live in, whilst accessing His humanity and divinity.

'Relational God' has been written from a deep desire to connect the reader with the reality of the Holiness of God. Her hope is that this is related in such a way that all who desire to know Him can find relationship and love throughout their life.